Software Asset Management

FOR
REFERENCE ONLY

OGC ITIL® Managing IT services

London: TSO

Published by TSO (The Stationery Office) and available from:

Online
www.tso.co.uk/bookshop

Mail, Telephone, Fax & E-mail
TSO
PO Box 29, Norwich, NR3 1GN
Telephone orders/General enquiries: 0870 600 5522
Fax orders: 0870 600 5533
E-mail: book.orders@tso.co.uk
Textphone 0870 240 3701

TSO Shops
123 Kingsway, London, WC2B 6PQ
020 7242 6393 Fax 020 7242 6394
68–69 Bull Street, Birmingham B4 6AD
0121 236 9696 Fax 0121 236 9699
9–21 Princess Street, Manchester M60 8AS
0161 834 7201 Fax 0161 833 0634
16 Arthur Street, Belfast BT1 4GD
028 9023 8451 Fax 028 9023 5401
18-19 High Street, Cardiff CF10 1PT
029 2039 5548 Fax 029 2038 4347
71 Lothian Road, Edinburgh EH3 9AZ
0870 606 5566 Fax 0870 606 5588

TSO Accredited Agents
(see Yellow Pages)

and through good booksellers

For further information on OGC products, contact:

OGC Service Desk
Rosebery Court
St Andrews Business Park
Norwich NR7 0HS
Telephone +44 (0) 845 000 4999

First published 2003
Second impression 2004
ISBN 0 11 330943 0

Printed in the United Kingdom for The Stationery Office
C7 05/04 ID168849 964067 19585

Titles within the ITIL series include:

Service Support (Published 2000)
Service Desk and the Process of Incident
Management, Problem Management, Configuration
Management, Change Management and
Release Management .... ISBN 0 11 330015 8

Service Delivery (Published 2001)
Capacity Management, Availability Management,
Service Level Management, IT Service Continuity,
Finanacial Management for IT Services and
Customer Relationship Management ... ISBN 0 11 330017 4

ICT Infrastructure Management .... ISBN 0 11 330865 5
Applications Management .... ISBN 0 11 330866 3
Planning to Implement Service Management ... ISBN 0 11 330877 9
Security Management .... ISBN 0 11 330014 X

ITIL back catalogue – an historical repository available as PDF downloads from www.tso.co.uk/ITIL

The managers' set
The complementary guidance set
Environmental management, strategy and computer operations set

■ CONTENTS

THE AUTHORS

Guidance was distilled from the experience of a range of people working in Software Asset Management (SAM), IT Service Management and/or ICT Infrastructure Management.

Colin Rudd, Director of IT Enterprise Management Systems Ltd (ITEMS), was the lead author. Colin has been working in the IT industry for over 30 years. He has been heavily involved in the development of the 'New ITIL', authoring or contributing to the production of many of the individual modules. He was also responsible for the design of the overall framework for the new library. Colin was recognised by the IT Service Management Forum (IT SMF), which is the IT Infrastructure Library (ITIL) user association, in 2002 with its lifetime service award for his work in the area of IT Service Management.

The project was managed by David Bicket, Senior Manager, Deloitte and Touche. David also contributed extensively to its design and writing.

Contributions to the content and the final Quality Assurance (QA) review were provided by Paul Diamond, Director, KPMG; Richard Bull, Manager, KPMG; Shaun Fröhlich, Chairman, Teksys Ltd; and Richard Best, Business Manager – Software Asset Management, Teksys Ltd.

In addition, a wide-ranging group of organisations participated in the overall QA process, including meetings, discussions of proposed contents, and reviewing drafts. Considerable time was required for this effort, against tight deadlines. Extensive thanks are due to all of those participating, who include:

Marina Schröder	Aspera OHG
Brian Davies	Barclays Bank PLC
Paul Noonan	Bytes Technology Group
Jenny Dugmore	ConnectSphere
Shirley Lacy	ConnectSphere and Chair, BCS Configuration Management Specialist Group
Eamonn McDonough	Department of Transport, UK Government
Barry Joyce	Hewlett Packard
Marianne Rinde	Hewlett Packard
Ronald B. Falciani	IBM Corporation
David Ward	IBM United Kingdom Ltd
David Phillips	Microsoft UK
Vaughan Smith	Microsoft UK
Wolfgang Bösing	Siemens Information & Communications Networks
David Gilchrist	Systems Management International
M. J. Perry	Vantico
Ronda Kiser	Whirlpool
David Nicoll	WPP
Denise E. Mason	Xansa

x

FOREWORD

Organisations are increasingly dependent on electronic delivery of services to meet Customer needs. This means a requirement for high quality IT services, matched to business needs and User requirements as they evolve.

OGC's ITIL (IT Infrastructure Library) is the most widely accepted approach to IT Service Management in the world. ITIL provides a cohesive set of best practice, drawn from the public and private sectors internationally, supported by a comprehensive qualification scheme, accredited training organisations, implementation and assessment tools.

Bob Assirati

OGC

PREFACE

The ethos behind the development of the IT Infrastructure Library (ITIL) is the recognition that organisations are increasingly dependent upon IT to satisfy their corporate aims and meet their business needs. This growing dependency leads to growing needs for quality IT services – quality that is matched to business needs and user requirements as they emerge. ITIL provides the guidance that will help to match that quality against the needs and cost in order to provide the best IT match for the business.

This is true no matter what type or size of organisation, be it national government, a multinational conglomerate, a decentralised office with either a local or centralised IT provision, an outsourced Service Provider, or a single office environment with one person providing IT support. In each case, there is the requirement to provide an economical service that is reliable, consistent and fit for purpose.

ICT Infrastructure Management is concerned with the processes, organisation and tools to provide a stable IT and communication infrastructure, and is the foundation for ITIL Service Management processes, promoting a quality approach to achieving business effectiveness and efficiency in the use of information systems. ITIL Service Management processes are intended to be implemented so that they underpin but do not dictate the business processes of an organisation. IT Service Providers will be striving to improve the quality of the service, but at the same time they will be trying to reduce the costs or, at a minimum, maintain costs at the current level.

For each of the ICT Infrastructure Management processes described in this book, one or more roles have been identified for carrying out the activities and producing the deliverables associated with the process. It should be recognised that it is often possible to allocate more than one role to an individual. Conversely, in larger organisations, more than one individual may be required to fulfil a role. The purpose of a role, as described in this book, is to locate responsibility, not to suggest an organisation structure.

█ INTRODUCTION

Most organisations today are dependent for their continued operation upon Information Technology (IT), or Information and Communications Technologies (ICT) as it is increasingly being called. Software is the most critical element of ICT and most organisations make huge investments in software, whether internally developed or externally procured. However, organisations often do not invest commensurate effort into managing these software assets.

This guide has been developed to assist with understanding what Software Asset Management (SAM) is, and to explain what is required to perform it effectively and efficiently as identified in industry 'best practice'. These guidelines can be tailored to fit any organisation, regardless of size.

This guide should be of interest to anybody involved in the acquisition, development, operation, use or retirement of software within an organisation. It should be of particular interest to two types of individuals:

- Directors and other members of senior management with corporate governance responsibility, including responsibility for software assets and the risks associated with them. These individuals will be most concerned with this introductory chapter.

- Individuals responsible for investigating or implementing improved processes and systems for SAM. These individuals should be interested in the entire guide.

1.1 The IT Infrastructure Library

This guide is complementary to the core materials of the IT Infrastructure Library (ITIL) and is intended to be consistent with all of its principles and processes. ITIL is the most widely accepted approach to IT Service Management in the world. ITIL provides a comprehensive and consistent set of best practices for IT Service Management, promoting a quality approach to achieving business effectiveness and efficiency in the use of information systems.

The ITIL label is owned by the Office of Government Commerce (OGC) of the UK Government, and was initially developed to provide guidance to UK Government departments. It has subsequently achieved acceptance worldwide, and a number of software manufacturers' own methodologies are aligned with it. It is fast becoming a *de facto* standard used by some of the world's leading businesses. A British Standard (BS 15000) has also been developed that has close links with ITIL. This guide is closely aligned with BS 15000 and is also compliant with the ISO 9000 quality standard.

This guide may be used by organisations that are already committed to ITIL best practice approaches in all areas, and also by organisations that are adopting such guidance on a more limited basis. If this is the first ITIL guide to be used within an organisation then it is strongly recommended that more is learnt about the full range of guidance available from ITIL (see www.itil.co.uk and also the related user group website at www.itsmf.com).

SAM is part of overall IT Service Management, and must be understood in this context. The SAM database, for example, is logically part of the Configuration Management Database (CMDB) that supports all of IT Service Management. These interrelationships between SAM and all of IT Service Management as defined by ITIL are explained in Section 1.11 and, in more detail, in Chapter 9. There is also repeated reference to other Service Management areas throughout this guide. The terminology used in this guide is consistent, to the extent practical, with terminology throughout the rest of ITIL, whilst also retaining consistency with software industry terminology.

1.2   What is SAM?

Software Asset Management means different things to different people. The definition used within this guide is as set out in the box.

> **Definition**
>
> Software Asset Management (SAM) is all of the infrastructure and processes necessary for the effective management, control and protection of the software assets within an organisation, throughout all stages of their lifecycle.

SAM does not include Hardware Asset Management, which will not be covered within this guide except for those aspects that are necessary for effective SAM. (Collectively, Software Asset Management and Hardware Asset Management can be referred to as IT Asset Management, or ITAM.) Generally speaking, SAM is more complex and more demanding than Hardware Asset Management and therefore the SAM processes need to be greater in scope and more comprehensive in content. As a result, systems that can handle SAM can normally be expected to handle Hardware Asset Management as well. Furthermore, it must be stressed that it is essential for hardware assets to be managed as well as software assets, even though not covered by this guide.

The coverage in this guide is intended to be manufacturer and platform neutral, to the extent practical. Specific products are not mentioned, nor is there focus on specific architectures such as mainframe or client/server. Most of the coverage should be equally applicable to PC workstations as to servers and mainframes, and even to network communications equipment such as routers.

1.3   The need for SAM

The underlying justification for SAM is the need to apply good corporate governance to an organisation's software assets. These typically include much of an organisation's asset base, are critical to its continued operations, and underlie some of an organisation's main legal and contractual obligations. This is a common-sense justification, but it is increasingly being reinforced by statutory or regulatory corporate governance requirements, such as Turnbull in the UK and Sarbanes-Oxley in the US. Consequently, the ultimate responsibility for good corporate governance of software assets lies with an organisation's senior management, and success or failure in this area ultimately rests with them.

> The importance of SAM is illustrated by a quote from George Cox, the Director General of the Institute of Directors (IoD) in the UK:
>
> 'The role and importance of externally acquired software has changed dramatically in recent years, to the point now where it has to be regarded as a business asset and managed as such. Software Asset Management has become an imperative, not an option. Software licences are business assets. Without them directors expose their business and themselves to constraints and to legal and financial risk.'

There is also a broader justification for SAM, which is all of the benefits it helps to deliver. Further detail about these is given in Section 1.5.

1.4 SAM principles

The overall objective of all SAM processes is that of good corporate governance, namely, the management of an organisation's software assets, including the management of the risks arising from the use of those assets.

> **The objective of SAM**
>
> To manage, control, and protect an organisation's software assets, including management of the risks arising from the use of those software assets.

A scaleable, structured approach needs to be adopted in order to achieve this for each organisation. The sequencing of the events involved in this structured approach is illustrated in Figure 1.1.

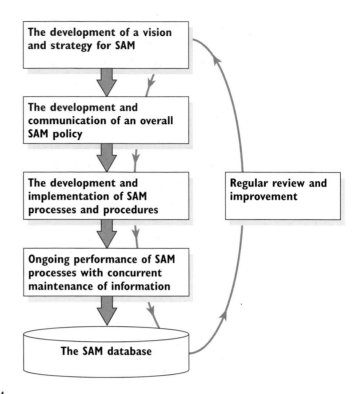

Figure 1.1 – The principles of SAM

The most important requirement for a SAM project is to have a clear vision and strategy that are owned by senior management. They should be the driver for initiating everything else in SAM, and in particular they drive the processes of creating the business case. This area is discussed in Chapter 3. This vision and strategy should include any overarching vision and strategy for Configuration Management as a whole, i.e. for all of ICT and not limited just to SAM.

Overall policies need to be established and communicated effectively to the entire organisation. Corresponding responsibilities also need to be clarified and communicated. These issues are addressed in several places throughout this guide, including in Chapter 4 'Organisation, Roles and Responsibilities', Section 5.1 'Overall Management Processes', and Appendix G 'Example Contents of a Software Policy'.

Detailed processes need to be defined and implemented, including automated capabilities and written procedures. The majority of the content of this guide addresses this area, including, in particular, Chapter 5 'Process Overview' and Chapter 6 'Implementation Overview'.

Key messages

■ Board-level sponsorship and commitment is essential to ensure successful SAM

■ Policies and procedures that are practical and mandatory for everyone touching IT assets (procurement to retirement) must be developed, implemented and monitored for adherence.

Once SAM is implemented, there will be ongoing performance of SAM processes with concurrent maintenance of information in the set of SAM databases (which is part of the

Configuration Management Database or CMDB in ITIL terminology) that will need to be tackled. SAM should be subject to the same disciplines of Service Management as all ICT services and infrastructure, as discussed in the core ITIL publications. For example, SAM cannot continue to function properly without attention to areas such as continuity of operations and Capacity Management. However, these more general topics are not discussed in detail in this guide.

The basis of any good SAM system is accurate and up-to-date SAM information, together with the processes for control of its accuracy. The SAM databases also provide essential information for the integration of SAM processes with other ICT and business processes. They should be considered logically as a single database, but may consist of several physically separate, but linked, databases. In highly decentralised organisations, each autonomous unit may have its own autonomous database, but there needs to be central collection of some data to achieve some of the greatest benefits of SAM. This area is discussed more in Chapter 4 'Organisation, Roles and Responsibilities'.

There also needs to be a regular process of review and improvement affecting all areas already addressed. At one level there should be review for compliance with defined policies and procedures and, where appropriate, corrective action. There may be opportunities for improvements in efficiency and effectiveness, and definitions of responsibilities. Vision may also change, perhaps in response to changing market opportunities and threats or technological developments. These issues are briefly addressed in Section 5.1 'Overall Management Processes', but repeating the entire process described above, at least for review purposes, is necessary periodically.

> **Key message**
>
> It is impossible to implement an effective SAM process without the successful design, development, implementation and maintenance of accurate SAM databases, automatically updated from the live infrastructure.

1.5 Benefits

The potential benefits of well-implemented SAM are significant and should usually greatly exceed the implementation and operating costs. There are many ways of categorising these benefits. Paragraphs 1.5.1–1.5.4 list the most significant benefits experienced by many organisations.

1.5.1 Managing risks

SAM facilitates the management of significant business risks including:

- **Legal and financial exposure:** There is risk to the organisation if licensing terms for externally procured software are not properly observed. This exposure may arise from enforcement agencies directly (e.g. police or customs), from industry associations (e.g. Business Software Alliance (BSA) or Federation Against Software Theft (FAST)) or from software manufacturers. It may be initiated by tip-offs from disgruntled employees (whistle blowers – potentially for a reward of *circa* £10k); by supplier knowledge (e.g. the reseller that fails to get a contract knowing the competitor's pricing cannot include licences); by software manufacturer analyses of customer purchasing; or by 'accident' (e.g. a police sweep through an entire building requiring companies to prove their licences). The characteristics of externally acquired software assets underlie these major exposures. Further detail is given in Section 2.1. In summary, the characteristics of commercial software assets underlie the following major exposures:

- software being resident/installed without licences being purchased
- loss of proof of licences which have been purchased, including licences underlying upgrades
- complex terms and conditions which may be breached unknowingly
- incorrect reliance on resellers.

■ **Damaged reputation:** An organisation's reputation may be damaged by the publicity that results if legal problems become publicly known. Likewise, an ICT department's reputation may be damaged within the organisation and within the ICT community if it experiences major unexpected problems related to the control of software assets, e.g. licensing, roll-outs, or support.

■ **Unexpected financial and workload impact:** Problems related to software assets, e.g. licensing, can have significant unexpected financial impact in areas such as cash flow, which can then impact on other planned activity. Likewise, ad hoc efforts to address licensing issues in response to external events can require major unplanned amounts of time from management and operational personnel, regardless of whether there is any ultimate direct financial impact.

■ **Security breaches including unauthorised disclosure of confidential information:** Security may be breached, and confidential information may be disclosed because of failure to implement adequate measures for security patch distribution.

Key message

'About 95% of exploits occur after bulletins and patches are put out … the reason the exploit is effective is because the patch uptake is too low.' *The chief security strategist for a major software manufacturer*

■ **Unexpected problems with acquisitions/mergers/demergers:** Failure to address SAM issues properly including licensing during 'due diligence' activity for acquisitions/mergers/demergers can expose the organisation to significant unexpected financial risk and operational impact.

■ **Interruption of operations:** The problems caused by poor SAM can sometimes affect continuity of operations, e.g. shutdowns caused by legal reasons, virus infections, or poorly deployed software updates. Conversely, good SAM can mitigate problems that might otherwise affect operations severely, e.g. being able to deploy security patches more quickly.

■ **Unsupportable operations:** There can be a risk of certain software-dependent operations being unsupportable without good SAM. For example, there may be critical applications reliant upon unlicensed software that ceases to be available for sale, preventing the possibility of continuing to use it while becoming compliant. Likewise, software manufacturers may cease upgrade and technical support for some products. Good SAM processes and related management planning should minimise such exposures.

1.5.2 Controlling costs

Proper SAM allows for significant cost savings, not only in direct expenditure on software, but also in related process and infrastructure costs. Some specific ways in which cost control can be improved as a result of good SAM are:

- **Better negotiating position:** Knowing with certainty that an organisation is compliant with licensing terms and conditions gives it a strong negotiating position with software manufacturers. Conversely, if there is a lack of clarity about the correctness of licensing, the reseller or software manufacturer may use that uncertainty to its negotiating advantage, with the possibility of a software audit being threatened to help close a deal that may not be in the organisation's best interest.

- **Improved strategic infrastructure planning:** Better knowledge about what is being installed/used, and better deployment capabilities, will facilitate the assessment of strategic software alternatives. For example, it is common for multinational companies to find dominant usage of one software manufacturer's products, with small pockets of competitive products that can typically be replaced under existing agreements at little or no additional cost. Alternatively, it will be easier to plan major infrastructure changes, including to competitive products.

- **Prevention of software over-deployment:** Proper SAM will help identify where software is needed, rather than just where it is installed, e.g. by monitoring active usage. A common finding is that standard configurations as installed are over-specified compared to what end-users actively use. Better identification of end-user needs can significantly reduce software and hardware requirements and costs as a result. Pull technology can allow for real-time deployment according to end-user requirements without the costs of comprehensive global deployments. Existing software investment will not be eliminated, but future costs may be greatly reduced by controlled redeployment of released licences. This information can also be important for negotiating major software agreements.

- **Reduced hardware costs**: Just as proper SAM can help prevent over-deployment of software, it will also help identify over-deployment of hardware. It can also facilitate the identification of other major opportunities for hardware savings, such as server consolidation, and time-phased purchasing requirements, which can be used in some cases to negotiate significant supplier cost savings.

- **Improved software purchasing arrangements:** A common finding, especially with large organisations, is that there are multiple purchasing points often making poor or no use of centrally arranged volume purchasing agreements for software. In these cases, the organisation could often achieve significantly better pricing if global purchasing arrangements covered all purchases.

- **Reduced costs of internal licensing support:** One of the most significant hidden costs of SAM is the cost of developing and maintaining licensing expertise amongst management and operational personnel, which in any case is often done inadequately with the attendant risks that result. By providing centralised skilled resources with licensing knowledge the corresponding hidden costs at local levels can be greatly reduced, and the risk of mistakes though lack of proper knowledge can also be minimised.

■ **Reductions in process and direct infrastructure costs:** There are clear savings that can be achieved in many areas as a result of good SAM implementations. For example:

- Well-designed infrastructure processes, working with accurate information about software assets, will function more efficiently, e.g. for roll-outs and upgrades
- Organisations will have Software Asset Management costs whether they formally recognise them or not. Savings can be expected if common solutions to Asset Management requirements can be implemented throughout the organisation instead of via independent ad hoc approaches, as is often the case.

■ **Reductions in problem-resolution costs:** A well-run ICT infrastructure, including proper SAM, should result in fewer operational problems with their attendant impacts, cost and otherwise. Likewise, a well-run ICT infrastructure should allow for faster and more cost-effective resolutions of those problems that do occur.

■ **Potential tax benefits:** Focus on tax issues, such as accelerated depreciation of some software expenditures, may result in significant tax benefits. (These may depend on many factors, such as the country, the industry, and the organisation's tax position.)

1.5.3 Obtaining competitive advantage

Proper SAM gives the organisation competitive advantage in several major ways:

■ **Better quality decision-making:** More accurate data on software assets, more readily available, allows for better quality management. In particular, good SAM improves transparency in overall ICT Management. For example, in a large organisation with many business units with their own ICT support structures, SAM can provide the transparency to help ensure that all ICT planning is assessed against common criteria, e.g. for renewal of assets, rather than on the basis of the forcefulness of the individual ICT managers.

■ **Faster time to market:** Proper SAM gives the organisation the ability to roll out improved ICT functionality faster but still with proper control. As a result, initiatives can be implemented more quickly, and reaction to changes in markets or competition can be faster, to give the organisation competitive advantage. Conversely, poor SAM may give the competitive advantage to others.

■ **Faster and easier integration after mergers and acquisitions:** Having proper SAM, and the ability to implement it quickly in new units, can facilitate the integration of organisations after mergers and acquisitions. The faster the ICT integration can be achieved, the sooner the anticipated benefits of the business combination should be achieved.

1.5.4 Enhancing employee motivation and the workplace environment

Proper SAM helps combat some of the main contributors to employee dissatisfaction, namely repeated ICT problems, and excessive delays in implementing new functionality. This can be particularly important for ICT support personnel who otherwise spend considerable time 'fire-fighting' without experiencing management support for their efforts.

Example

A large multinational that had just completed the implementation of SAM was approached by one of its software manufacturers with the threat of a licensing audit. The Chief Information Officer (CIO) knew exactly how much of that software manufacturer's software was being used, and where, and even knew that there was overlicensing because of changing ICT infrastructures. The CIO immediately agreed to the audit, but the software manufacturer never conducted it. The CIO's improved view of software usage allowed him to achieve significant cost savings with that software manufacturer and most other software manufacturers as well. Significant savings on planned future hardware expenditures were also achieved.

1.6 The possible problems

Some of the potential problems that may arise related to SAM include the following, many of which are similar to the problems of all system initiatives, but some of which have particular relevance to SAM.

1.6.1 Conflict with decentralisation culture

A common management philosophy is 'small is beautiful', with heavy reliance on decentralisation to stimulate initiative and innovation. This philosophy may work in many areas, but has significant limitations in the area of SAM because many of the significant procurement benefits are achieved by centralisation, and many of the related risks are best managed on a centralised basis. Conversely, decentralised ICT Management approaches can create global risk for the organisation because software manufacturers and legal authorities will not differentiate to suit the management approach if there are individual units that are seen as violating licensing terms and conditions. A comparison can be made with treasury functions, e.g. for capital expenditure. Even in highly decentralised organisations, this function tends to be centralised or have strong central oversight. SAM needs to be treated in a similar fashion.

1.6.2 Lack of senior management support

Successful SAM implementation is much more than the implementation of a tool. It will typically require significant culture change, which can only be achieved with active senior management support. It may be hard to get that support for a variety of reasons, e.g. SAM is not the current management fad, or SAM is not seen as being exciting. It is, instead, a 'nuts and bolts' function that underpins the successful management of software and with it the operational infrastructure of the organisation. Proper senior management support will result in sufficient budget, resources, knowledge and skills being allocated to SAM implementation and ongoing operation.

1.6.3 Lack of clear responsibilities

An implementation project without clearly assigned responsibilities, both for the project and for ongoing responsibilities after implementation, will likely fail. In practice, it may be difficult to define responsibilities clearly, e.g. when there are already grey areas between group ICT and business unit ICT responsibilities, and when there are existing outsourcing agreements and Service Level Agreements (SLAs) with responsibilities already defined or excluded.

1.6.4 Imbalance between 'customised' and 'off-the-shelf' software perspectives

There is a point of view sometimes expressed that software must always be chosen and tailored to meet an organisation's unique requirements. This approach can easily be taken to unjustifiable extremes. An organisation's requirements should certainly be determined before selecting software. However, if those requirements cannot easily be met using existing software packages without customisation, then the requirements should be reassessed. Otherwise, there is a strong risk of software being customised to meet inflexible and poorly thought-out requirements which would result in a costly solution supplied late which does not meet real SAM requirements. Such a solution may represent a bureaucratic and inflexible view of control. By analogy, an organisation that custom-designs its accounting software to meet existing accounting procedures is normally asking for disaster. Unfortunately, the SAM tools available do not yet have the degree of maturity of current accounting and logistical systems, where most major packages provide similar and generally accepted functionality. Current 'best practice' in the SAM area is to use a combination of available tools but without extensive customisation. This area will clearly continue to develop.

1.6.5 Underestimating the effort required to identify installed software

It is common to underestimate the amount of time and effort required to turn detailed discovery information into useful information about installed applications. There may be thousands of files associated with a single application or licence. Different combinations may indicate partial installs, full installs or incomplete uninstalls, and there may be different levels of updates or security patches to identify. The demands escalate if in-house and non-commercial software is included in the analysis. The tool(s) selected, and possibly the partner selected to help implement/use the tool(s), can be important in controlling time and effort in this area.

1.6.6 Legal requirements

Implementing SAM, especially for a multinational organisation, may require unexpected amounts of effort to comply with local legislation. Particular consideration should be given to data protection issues (confidentiality of personal information, transmission of personal information across borders, etc.). In some countries, there may also be a requirement to consult local employee organisations, e.g. a Works Council. Some types of metering, in particular, may be viewed as employee monitoring, and may need careful discussion.

1.6.7 Lack of end-user support

End-users typically will not support a new system unless they see it being actively supported by senior management, and unless they see a direct personal benefit from it. End-users need to see SAM and ICT in general as being responsive to their needs, and minimising problems and hassle.

1.6.8 Lack of communication

If ICT staff and the user community are not made aware of the organisation's software policy and of their roles and responsibilities with regard to the use of software assets, then the enforcement of SAM processes within an organisation is difficult.

Example

A large travel organisation was starting SAM implementation with adequate people and resources committed to the project. However, overall ownership was not agreed and people's roles and responsibilities within the implementation of the SAM processes were not clearly defined, documented and agreed. The result was that much time was wasted, the project was delayed and almost cancelled due to these issues before remedial actions were taken.

Key message

Ensure that sponsorship, ownership, terms of reference, scope, processes, roles and responsibility are clearly defined in the early stages of SAM implementation.

1.7 Costs

The implementation of SAM will inevitably incur costs. The scale of these costs will depend in part on the implementation approach chosen (see Section 1.8), and also on other factors such as:

- the size, culture and structure of the organisation involved
- the level of senior management sponsorship and commitment to SAM within the organisation
- the size, scope and timescale of the proposed project
- the current use of technology and software within the organisation
- the current state and maturity of the SAM processes within the organisation
- the tools to be used and the level of automation planned
- the degree to which a customised solution is wanted vs. the willingness to use existing/available tools and systems that may not meet all perceived requirements (see Section 1.6)
- the SAM skills, resources and knowledge within the organisation
- the number of devices in use, e.g. mainframe, mid, desktops, servers etc.

The main costs will be incurred within the following areas:

- **People:** People will be required to develop and perform the roles and activities required within the SAM processes, both during their implementation and their subsequent ongoing operation. This may require the involvement of senior management, project managers, external partners and consultants where the skills, knowledge and availability of internal resources are not suitable.
- **Tools:** Both hardware and software may need to be selected, implemented, configured and tailored to automate aspects of the SAM processes.

11

- **Interfaces:** These may need to be developed.
- **Corrective licences:** There may be additional costs to make up for any identified shortfalls in software licences.

Key message

The costs associated with the implementation of SAM may seem extensive, even prohibitive. However, intelligent exploitation of existing infrastructure, processes and tools should help to contain costs. A good SAM implementation should typically bring significant financial savings within a year of completion.

SAM costs should furthermore be seen as necessary expenditure to control the many software-related risks faced by the organisation.

1.8 Implementation approaches

The implementation of SAM within an organisation is an extensive and demanding task. There are many different approaches that can be adopted which generally fall into three different categories:

- **Internal project:** This involves the use of resources from within the organisation to implement the SAM processes. It is the preferred approach if the necessary SAM skills and knowledge are present and available within the organisation. It should involve the use of an approved organisational project methodology, e.g. PRINCE2.
- **Partnership project:** This involves the use of an external partner or partner(s) to assist with the implementation of SAM. This approach has distinct advantages where there is a lack of either internal skills or resources within the required SAM timescale.
- **Outsourced project or managed service:** This involves contracting an external organisation or partner to implement the complete activity.

It is critically important if the complete activity is outsourced that the client still takes ownership of the strategy and makes decisions on information provided. Any outsourced contract should be on the basis of Key Performance Indicators (KPIs) that require the supplier to manage effectively the assets, i.e. not payments based on numbers of assets managed. Otherwise, there is no incentive to dispose of assets not required by the business.

These approaches can be applied not only to the implementation of SAM processes but also to their continued operation.

The approach selected by an individual organisation will depend upon many factors, including overall cost, the demands for 'business as usual', and the availability of budget and other required resources.

1.9 Minimum implementation recommendations

Smaller organisations, especially ones that have not already embraced ITIL, may find the extensive coverage of this guide more than they are seeking initially. It is strongly recommended that somebody be given the responsibility for developing an appropriate SAM strategy for each organisation, and that reading this entire guide should be one of the required tasks. This being said, this section summarises the most significant recommendations that all organisations should expect to implement, regardless of size.

1.9.1 Overall baseline recommendations

The following list is the suggested minimum set of recommendations for Software Asset Management in any size or type of organisation:

- **Vision:** Senior management should determine why SAM is needed in a way that aligns with the overall organisational vision and objectives. The vision ideally should include other ITIL service areas as well (see Section 3.1).

- **Decision about centralisation:** Determine the degree of centralisation to be required in SAM. Some of the most significant benefits of SAM come from centralisation of expertise, procurement and Risk Management functions, regardless of the degree of decentralisation of other functions. It is a similar situation to capital expenditure control (see Section 4.1).

- **Responsibilities and policies:** Establish clear overall responsibilities and policies for SAM commensurate with the decision on centralisation. Responsibilities should include Risk Management such as for contractual and legal risks. Policies should make clear the obligations of all officers, employees and contractors and the consequences of violations (see Section 4.4, Paragraph 5.1.3 and Appendix G).

- **Skills and competence:** Develop and maintain strong SAM skills including software licensing. Read and understand software licensing contracts, with particular focus on volume licensing contracts that give audit rights to software manufacturers. If reliance is being placed on an outside organisation, that organisation must provide input into all necessary SAM processes, and not just advice on licences for new software being purchased. Remember also that legal exposures cannot be contracted out, so there must be enough internal competence to ensure adequate controls over these exposures (see Paragraph 5.1.4).

- **Detailed strategy**: Develop clear statements of detailed ICT strategy. Standardisation of common software and of deployment configurations is of particular importance for overall cost reduction (see ITIL Guide to ICT Infrastructure Management).

- **Contracting**: Choose appropriate partners, including for the supply of software. Ensure that software purchasing arrangements are structured to minimise cost whilst still ensuring control. For example, global contracts typically give the best pricing, but reporting of usage should be at a lower level (e.g. by country, subsidiary or business unit) to facilitate reconciliations and control (see Chapter 8, Paragraph 5.5.1 and Appendix E).

- **Procedures:** Establish robust procurement, deployment and retirement procedures that ensure compliance with policies and which themselves capture necessary information and assets, especially proof of licence (see Paragraphs 5.3.4, 5.3.6 and 5.3.9).

- **Inventories:** Create and maintain accurate inventories of software and hardware assets including costs, with secure control over access to software assets, e.g. proof of licence, and distribution copies of software (see Paragraph 5.2.1 and Appendix D).

- **Reconciliations:** Perform regular reconciliations of (a) what is actually installed against (b) what is recorded against (c) licences owned (for licensed software), and resolve any identified exceptions promptly. The frequency of the reconciliations will depend on the effectiveness of procedures for accurate record-keeping and Licence Management, but should not be less than yearly. Some organisations do this on a continuous automated basis (see Section 5.4).

- **Cost/benefit analysis:** Develop, collect and utilise relevant data for ICT procurement decision-making about total cost of ownership (TCO) including benefits, both quantified and non-quantified (see Paragraph 5.2.5).

1.9.2   National Audit Office recommendations

The Comptroller and Auditor General in the UK is the head of the National Audit Office (NAO) and reports to Parliament. He certifies the accounts of all Government departments and a wide range of other public sector bodies, and can report on the economy, efficiency and effectiveness with which departments and other bodies have used their resources. He issued a report on 1 May 2003 on 'Purchasing and Managing Software Licences' (www.nao.gov.uk, report HC 579) with a number of recommendations that can be considered minimum best procurement practice for UK Government organisations. A comparable generic recommendation is made by this guide for all organisations. This is effectively a specialised subset of the baseline recommendations given in Paragraph 1.9.1.

Table 1.1 – NAO and generic recommendations for purchasing and managing software licences.

	NAO recommendations for UK Government departments © UK National Audit Office	*Generic recommendations for all organisations*
	For departments	*For all organisations with direct purchasing responsibility for software assets*
1	Maintain reliable information to assess the extent of their expenditure on software and supporting licences	Same
2	Consider in the first instance using the Memoranda of Understanding negotiated by OGC with suppliers	Consider in the first instance centralised purchasing arrangements
3	Check regularly to ensure that no unlicensed software is being used on their systems	Same
4	Consider the total cost of ownership when purchasing major upgrades or new systems	Same
	For the Office of Government Commerce	*For group/corporate ICT procurement functions*
5	Monitor carefully take-up of the Memoranda of Understanding and the discounts received by departments	Monitor decentralised use of centralised purchasing arrangements and benefits achieved

1.10   World-class SAM

For those organisations that are implementing more than just the minimum, the question is how far to go. Metrics in this area are limited. However, there does appear to be at least one differentiator of what can be considered 'world-class SAM' – the types of software covered by SAM implementation. The first approach (which most organisations implement with SAM) is to provide version control and implementation confirmation (or copy control) of 'standard' software. The second (which far fewer organisations implement successfully) covers all software including in-house applications and non-commercial software such as Internet file-swapping applications. The second gives better Risk Management, but the first is adequate as a procurement tool.

1.11   How SAM maps to ITIL

The relationship between SAM and the modules within ITIL is illustrated in Figure 1.2.

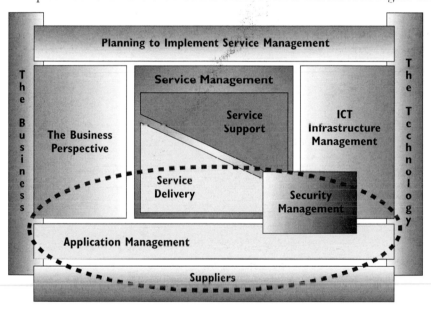

■ ■ ■ The scope of Software Asset Management (SAM)

Figure 1.2 – Relationship between SAM and the ITIL framework

The individual areas can be briefly described as follows:

- **Planning to Implement Service Management** covers the planning of Service Management processes, together with the development of organisational and ICT cultures.

- **Service Management** consists of two guides:
  - **Service Delivery** covers the processes associated with the development and improvement of the quality of ICT services delivered to the business, consisting of Service Level Management (SLM), Financial Management, Capacity Management, IT Service Continuity Management and Availability Management.
  - **Service Support** describes the function and processes involved in the day-to-day support and maintenance of ICT services, consisting of Incident Management,

Problem Management, Configuration Management, Change Management and Release Management and the Service Desk function.

- *ICT Infrastructure Management* describes all of the processes associated with the management of the ICT Infrastructure, including overall management, Design and Planning, Deployment, Operations and Technical Support.

- *Application Management* includes all of the processes and issues associated with the development and management of applications and software lifecycles.

- *Security Management* covers all of the processes and issues associated with the security of ICT services and systems.

- *Business Perspective* focuses on the processes of business alignment and communication associated with ICT systems and services.

The areas of ITIL that are associated with the operation of SAM processes are contained within the *Service Management*, *Security Management* and *Applications Management* ITIL guides. The *ICT Infrastructure Management* and *Business Perspective* areas are also involved but to a lesser extent. The management of contracts and suppliers is also a key area for both SAM and ITIL.

Further detailed information about the mapping of SAM to ITIL and other approaches is given in Chapter 9.

1.12   How this guide is organised

This guide is organised as indicated in Figure 1.3, which emphasises the four Ps:

- **Processes:** The management processes required for effective SAM (which is the emphasis of this guide).

- **People:** The people involved in SAM and their roles and responsibilities.

- **Products:** The management technology and tools used within the SAM processes.

- **Partners:** The other external organisations involved within SAM processes including manufacturers, resellers and SAM consultants.

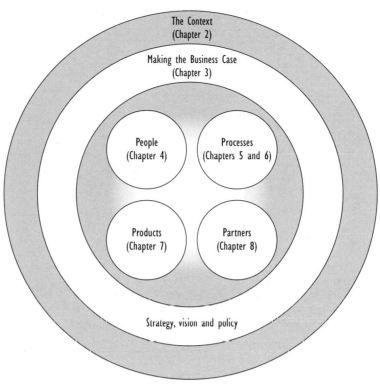

Figure 1.3 – The structure of this guide

Chapter 1 provides an overall introduction to SAM and Chapter 2 gives information about the context and the special nature of software assets. Chapter 3 provides advice on making the business case for SAM and covers the development of the vision and the strategy, with an example policy document included in Appendix G.

Chapter 4 covers some of the most important 'people' issues related to organisation, roles and responsibilities. Chapters 5 and 6 give information about SAM processes, and this is the main focus of the guide, including the creation and maintenance of the SAM database set. (Chapter 5 gives the details of SAM processes in live systems, including review, audit and improvement and Chapter 6 gives an overview of the implementation.) Chapter 7 covers 'products', i.e. the tools and technology. Chapter 8 covers the types of services available from partners.

Chapter 9 explains the mapping of SAM to ITIL and similar approaches. The appendices provide supporting materials, such as Appendix B, which contains an overview of software licensing.

2 CONTEXT

Software assets are essentially intellectual property assets. These types of asset have unique characteristics that differentiate them from the more common, purely physical assets. In order to appreciate the implications for SAM, it is useful to understand more about these unique characteristics, and about the industry that has generated the majority of software assets in use in the world today.

2.1 Special characteristics of software assets

There are many assets that ICT organisations need to manage, and software is just one of them. The major types of assets that need to be managed within ICT are:

- computer and network equipment
- environmental equipment
- buildings and facilities
- software assets
- data and databases
- processes and policies
- documentation and contracts
- people.

However, software is probably the most complex to manage, because of the complexity of its lifecycle. Furthermore, commercial software can have significant legal and financial risks associated with its special characteristics:

- **Risk of software being used without licences being purchased:**
  - Liability for licence payments typically can be incurred without going through a procurement process, but rather simply by installing/using the software, even if done without proper authorisation.
  - Even with proper authorisation, software installations may not be properly reported. This is because volume-licensing contracts typically allow for installation before 'reporting', i.e. before paying for the software. Reporting is honour-based, but with audit rights for the software manufacturer. Because there is no physical requirement to purchase a licence before using it, there is increased reliance on proper internal controls to ensure that reporting is correct. However, these are not typical controls for other areas of procurement, so there is significant risk that they will not be performed correctly.
- **Risk of the loss of proof of licences which have been purchased:**
  - Licences may be lost physically because the importance of proof of licence documentation is often not recognised, and therefore there may be a failure to keep them under any sort of control.
  - Licences may be lost 'administratively' because a central unit may perform purchasing, obtaining consolidated licences for all purchases which are then administratively difficult to tie back to the ordering units. Also, subsidiary units

that were licensed may then be sold or reorganised, and the licences will not move with them.

- Licences may be ordered via a reseller, but proper proof of licence may not be received from the software manufacturer. The reporting flow for volume purchases from an end-customer to the software manufacturer is largely one-way, without the usual inherent checks of physical purchases. The loop is typically closed only by the customer checking for the receipt of proper proof of licence from the software manufacturer. This is not a standard process for physical procurement processes, and consequently it may be omitted or performed poorly. As a result, proofs of licence that were paid for may never be received, and furthermore may not be recognised as missing.

■ **Risk of terms and conditions being breached unknowingly:**

- Externally procured software assets typically have complex legal conditions that can be misunderstood even by people working in the area.
- Software is frequently upgraded and licence conditions can change with upgrades.
- What constitutes 'proof of licence' can be a complex issue in itself. The issues surrounding this area are explained in Appendix B.

■ **Risk of incorrect reliance on resellers:**

- There is sometimes a tri-partite legal relationship between a software manufacturer, reseller and the customer that does not apply to most other assets. It is not possible to rely solely on the reseller. Each set of relationships needs to be properly managed. What a reseller says normally does not change the contractual obligations of the end-user organisation towards the software manufacturer.

A piece of software within the ICT environment may consist of all or some of the following components:

- ■ the master copy of the software itself on the master media
- ■ distribution copies of the software on free-standing media or on servers
- ■ the software licence certificates or other 'proof of licence'
- ■ terms and conditions of licence
- ■ support contracts
- ■ software pass codes or licence keys
- ■ software maintenance authorisation codes
- ■ the software release documentation
- ■ upgrade components
- ■ the installed operational instances of the software.

The management of software would therefore need to control all of these different aspects and would involve interfacing with many other ICT Asset Management processes and units.

2.2 Legal context

One of the main exposures with externally acquired software is the legal exposure that comes with use contrary to terms and conditions or legislation. The legal bases for this exposure depend on the country and contractual conditions, but mainly comprise of:

- copyright legislation
- trademark legislation
- contract law.

Key message

The protection and enforcement of intellectual property rights, including for software, is increasing worldwide. For example, UK legislation introduced in late 2002 provided for:

- confiscation of assets
- substantial late fees, and
- up to 10 years in jail

  or

- an unlimited fine.

Violations may be unintentional or intentional. Unintentional violations are common and may be caused by various factors:

- lack of understanding of licensing terms and conditions
- lack of records about software usage, and often not even knowing the number of PCs in use
- lack of robust ICT deployment procedures to ensure that all installations are properly authorised, including ensuring that necessary licences are procured
- purchase from or installation by suppliers of unlicensed or counterfeit software.

Although such violations may be unintentional, they are still violations. Furthermore, there is usually a 'duty of care' on the part of organisations for the way they conduct their business. Failure to focus on the issue of legal risk because of other priorities is unlikely to be an acceptable excuse with software manufacturers or in court.

Directors and other senior management may take several steps to reduce personal exposure to such violations. Ensuring that there are adequate systems of internal control in operation is an important factor, and good SAM processes help meet this requirement. It is also important to ensure that employees understand relevant policies and confirm this with signed statements, and that there are meaningful disciplinary measures in place for violations.

As mentioned above, the unknowing purchase from or installation by suppliers of unlicensed or counterfeit software is a major source of exposure to risk of litigation. This may occur for many reasons:

- **Lack of clarity between supplier and customer about the supply of licences:** A common problem can occur when a supplier provides hardware with software pre-installed, or when a supplier provides implementation support, e.g. for a system migration. Often the end-user organisation will assume that the supplier is providing the licences. The supplier, however, may assume that the customer is providing the licences, perhaps under an existing volume-licensing contract held by the customer. The customer is almost certainly responsible, unless the supplier has a clear contractual obligation to provide the licences. Even in this case, the customer has a 'duty of care' to ensure that appropriate proof of licence is received.

- **Counterfeit software:** There is a significant risk of receiving counterfeit software, including counterfeit media and 'proof of licence' especially with longer supply chains in which there is more opportunity for counterfeit products to enter the chain. This topic is covered more in Appendix B.

- **Hard-disk loading:** Hard-disk loading refers to the practice, more likely to be encountered amongst smaller suppliers, of putting software on customers' machines without supplying the corresponding media or licences. Often this will occur as part of the supply of hardware, e.g. on a new PC or server. Even if the software is mentioned on the invoice, this is normally not sufficient, and proper documentation of proof of licence is still required.

Examples

The scale of the issue

Over 6,500 European businesses were taken to court in 2001 for contravention of software copyright.

BSA studies estimate that *c*.25% of business software used in the UK is unlicensed.

BSA studies estimate that *c*.40% of business software used worldwide is unlicensed.

There have been many recent, high-profile examples of organisations contravening copyright laws, ranging from high street retailers, international banks, through local government to small and medium sized businesses. The penalties for these offences have ranged from a few thousand pounds to hundreds of thousands of pounds.

A national distributor with a chain of several hundred resellers had to recently pay an undisclosed sum of damages for activities over a number of years where it had been inadvertently distributing counterfeit copies of illegal software that it had purchased in good faith.

A study conducted in the late 1990s in one major country identified that more than twice as many PC motherboards were being supplied to the market by one hardware manufacturer alone compared to the number of operating systems purchased in total in that country.

There are also legal issues involved with the installation of software, because of the common practice of requiring a user to agree to licence terms and conditions as part of the installation process. Users typically will not bother to read these terms and conditions. In some cases, they include allowing the manufacturer to install and run other programs on the user's computer, e.g. for marketing purposes.

2.3   Software industry supply chain

The situation with regard to the sale and distribution of software is a complex one. There are many different organisations and players involved with the user organisation at the end of a long and sometimes complex chain. The onus is on the user organisation to ensure that the software provided is genuine. The roles of the main players within the software industry are as detailed in Figure 2.1 and in the following text:

- **Software Manufacturers/Vendors/Publishers:** These are responsible for providing quality software that is fit for purpose, together with all licensing information necessary for the operation and use of the software. Software remains the intellectual property of the manufacturer. All that is purchased is a licence to use the software.

- **Original Equipment Manufacturers (OEM):** These install software on their hardware and sell it on as a package. The licence for OEM software is typically with the OEM, and not with the software manufacturer (the main exception to that general rule). As a result, OEM licences are usually contractually bound to the hardware they are sold with, and are not transferable to other machines.

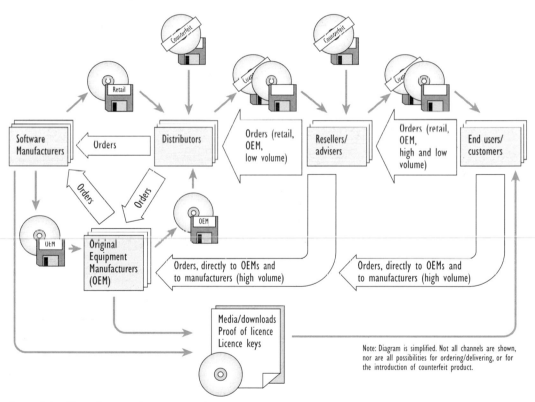

Figure 2.1 – The software industry supply chain

- **Distributors:** These normally do not deal directly with end-customers, but only with software manufacturers and resellers. They deal in very high volumes of software of low-volume types, e.g. retail products, low-volume programs, and OEM products. Some counterfeit products have entered the supply channel via (smaller) distributors.

- **Resellers:** These normally deal directly with end-customers, for most levels of software purchasing, e.g. retail, OEM, low-volume, and high-volume programs. Counterfeit products have entered the supply channel via resellers, more commonly via smaller resellers. Some software manufacturers have authorised resellers, with whom the risk of buying counterfeit products should be minimised.

■ **Advisers:** These assist customers in placing orders, but the contractual relationships are directly between the customer and the software manufacturer. The software manufacturer pays a fee to the adviser.

■ **End-user organisation:** The organisation ultimately purchases the licences, and has ultimate responsibility for ensuring that genuine proof of licence is received for all purchases made.

2.4 Other software industry players

There are several other types of industry player that should also be mentioned here. (See also Chapter 8 on 'Partners and SAM'.)

■ **Standards and professional organisations:** Organisations that provide professional guidance on the development and control of software and related services. Examples include:

- ITIL – the IT Infrastructure Library. See the preface to this guide for further explanation.
- British Standards Institute – the owners of BS 15000, the IT Service Management standard, and other standards.

■ **Anti-piracy organisations:** These are industry organisations that exist to ensure that software licensing requirements and national and international law on software usage are complied with. The three main organisations are:

- Business Software Alliance (BSA): An organisation active in many countries, with membership drawn from software manufacturers, varying sometimes by country. Amongst other activities, the BSA provides education on software copyright issues and guidance on how to conduct self-audits. It fights software piracy in many ways, including through enforcement activities.
- Software Publishers Alliance (SPA): A division of the Software & Information Industry Association (SIIA) that works in the areas of education and enforcement in dealing with software management and piracy.
- The Federation Against Software Theft (FAST): A UK-based software anti-piracy organisation representing both software publishers and end-users. FAST has investigators and in-house lawyers who specialise in safeguarding software publishers' intellectual property. FAST also has a consultancy branch that helps UK organisations by providing guidance, training and education through its audit certification programme.

3 MAKING THE BUSINESS CASE

Successful implementation of SAM is dependent upon the establishment of a suitable culture within the organisation and the commitment and support of senior business and ICT managers. Neither of these is likely to happen unless a successful business case is produced and accepted by the senior management within the organisation.

> **Key message**
>
> Senior management and financial approval bodies are not primarily interested in technical arguments. To be successful, a business case must relate costs to business benefits, using sound methods of investment appraisal.

Each organisation will probably have its own standards and format for business cases. The business case prepared for SAM should follow organisational standards, and should be logical, well-structured and concise. Guidance on making business cases in general can be found elsewhere. This chapter focuses on making a successful business case specifically for SAM.

3.1 Develop a vision and strategy

Before developing a business case for SAM, consideration should be given to the overall vision and strategy of the project in business terms. It is best to align these clearly with an organisation's corporate or business strategy. Examples of the types of business and corporate strategies that SAM has been aligned to are:

- improving 'time to market' for products and services
- development of 'world-class' services and products
- creation of more market-competitive offerings
- driving down operating costs and increasing profitability
- ensuring staff have quality roles and jobs
- increasing business and employee productivity
- ensuring continuity of business processes
- managing business risks
- reducing the total cost of ownership (TCO) of ICT systems and services.

An alternative approach is also possible, related to personal Risk Management for senior officers. Often senior management and directors assume that all risks associated with the use of software within the organisation have been appropriately addressed by ICT Management. Unfortunately, this is often not the case and the senior managers or directors, who are ultimately responsible for SAM, may be unaware of the vulnerabilities, business impacts and penalties potentially associated with poor control over software assets. Increasingly in many countries, individual directors and other officers may be held personally responsible for problems arising from areas for which they are responsible, whether they are exercising active control or not. To minimise personal exposure to risk, senior management and directors need to ensure that there are adequate systems of control in place over software assets.

Example

The need for SAM was forcibly brought to the attention of one global
organisation when their offices in an Asian country were searched by the local
police force. The police were systematically sweeping through multi-storey
buildings floor by floor and arrived at the floors occupied by this organisation.
Panic struck the local employees when the police refused to accept that the
organisation had worldwide agreements for software, and demanded to see licence
documents for the software on each individual PC.

As a result of this incident, SAM became a strategic issue for this organisation.
However, SAM strategy should be developed proactively rather than reactively!

Vision and strategy also grow from seeing what other organisations accomplish. To date, there has
been comparatively little formal analysis and reporting of the benefits of SAM, and this is
undoubtedly a factor in its limited visibility on senior management 'radar screens'. But evidence is
accumulating. As part of an organisation's approach to a SAM project, feedback should be sought
from other organisations that have successfully implemented SAM, and the benefits achieved.
Some examples of real-world results are given below.

Examples of savings made through SAM

Note: The examples cited here are not considered extreme cases, but realistic
examples of what is achievable. The savings in each case were dependent on the
specific circumstances of the organisations involved, and of the licensing
programs/pricing relevant for them at the time, and may not be relevant for others.
Although the specific opportunities will differ for each organisation, it is likely that
the ones available will be significant but they must be recognised and acted on.
Most of the benefits cited here relate to savings in costs of licensing, which are
often the easiest to identify. However, licensing is only a small part of TCO, and
the savings in other areas may easily be much larger, although often harder to
identify and measure.

- A multi-national organisation had a decentralised approach to the negotiation
  of software licences. This resulted in the overbuying of licences, and poor
  pricing. By centralising the process of software licence negotiation and dealing
  often directly with the software suppliers and publishers, more cost-effective
  licence agreements were obtained for the organisation as a whole, saving in
  excess of an estimated five million dollars.

- A major organisation needed to upgrade its software. Prior to implementing
  SAM, its best alternative was to purchase a site agreement covering usage on
  all machines. After a major exercise to determine what licences it really
  owned, it determined it could purchase primarily upgrade licences, achieving
  the upgrade objective at only 46% of the cost of the site agreement.

- A review of software maintenance contracts at another organisation revealed
  that maintenance was continuing to be paid on software that was no longer
  being used. The contracts were cancelled at a saving of over half a million
  euros.

> - A major company with a comparatively low PC:employee ratio found that it could reduce its need for Client Access Licences (CALs) by 45%, by switching from calculating CALs on a per-person basis to a per-PC basis.
>
> - Another organisation found that it could reduce existing licence usage requirements by 3% by removing software from PCs where it was not being used actively, allowing licences to be redeployed elsewhere.

3.2 Investigate the issues

3.2.1 Determine requirements

The first stage of the development of any business case is the requirements-gathering and documentation stage. This can be achieved using well-established techniques such as:

- interviews with representatives from the business, including users, customers and managers
- written questionnaires
- software industry reports and information from consultants and specialists
- user groups and industry forum reports and seminars
- industry and customer surveys
- risk assessments.

Key message

Many projects fail to deliver benefits, as the business objectives were not clearly established at the outset, making it difficult to get buy-in from the business and the end-users.

The most essential part of this stage is to gather information on:

- Benefits that are priority objectives of a SAM project (see Section 1.4):
  - risks that need to be addressed by the project – these include, for example, damage to reputation if there is negative publicity about underlicensing
  - cost savings
  - competitive advantage
  - workplace enrichment.

- The potential stakeholders and sponsors of the project and their expectations and reasons for actively supporting and driving the project to a successful conclusion.

- Management attitudes towards key SAM implementation decisions that will need to be made:
  - acceptable degree of centralisation of SAM functions (see Section 4.1)
  - acceptable degree of centralisation of the SAM database (see Section 4.2).

- The potential objections to the project and measures to counter these:
  - 'It is compliance driven, but not worth having for positive benefits.'
  - 'We have existed without it for years, why do it now?'
  - 'Asset Management is not a priority; there are more important things to do.'
  - 'The idea is too bureaucratic and not workable.'
  - 'People won't accept new processes and working practices.'
  - 'The SAM tool market is immature with no fully comprehensive or integrated solutions yet available.'

- The functionality required by the solution. This should be categorised as functionality that is either essential, important or 'nice to have'.
- The performance levels required by the solution: KPIs and other metrics.
- The current state of SAM activities.

3.2.2 Analyse the gap

Once the basic information has been gathered, a gap analysis should be performed between what is currently being achieved, and what is required/desired.

3.2.3 Identify and analyse alternatives

There are likely to be a significant number of implementation alternatives, depending on factors such as those described in Sections 1.7 and 1.8. Each alternative should be assessed for its expected costs, benefits and timescales, as well as associated risks of failure.

The viable alternatives should be compared on an appropriate basis (which may be required by company policy), probably including TCO and calculations of Return on Investment (ROI), and a decision made as to the preferred alternative.

3.3 Document the business case

The formal documentation of the business case should follow the organisation's own requirements. Generally, it should be expected to include:

- executive summary and recommendation as to preferred implementation alternative
- business requirements and benefits expected
- alternatives considered
- business impacts of each alternative: benefits, costs, risks
- recommended implementation plan
- expected realisation of benefits plan (time-phased achievement of benefits).

Key message

Many business cases lack support and are rejected because they fail to relate to strategic business objectives and benefits, but concentrate on ICT and technological excellence. The key to the acceptance of a business case is to align the project visions and goals with strategic business visions and goals and to show an ROI. An example strategy for SAM is:

'To provide world-class ICT services to all customers, both internal and external, by ensuring responsive, effective, cost-efficient and legal exploitation of software assets.'

3.4 Sell the business case

Selling the business case is as important – or more so – as physically preparing it. In principle, everything that is done during the preparation of the business case is part of selling it. For example, while determining requirements it will be possible to identify people's objections and to start to counter them and convince people of the benefits that can be achieved.

A senior-level champion must be found early in the process. Without such a champion, it will be difficult to achieve the management support necessary for the real change throughout the organisation required for a successful implementation of SAM. Achieving budgetary approval is not enough.

The selling must also continue after the business case is approved. People who initially were not interested may become interested, but negatively. It will be better to take the time to convince them of the benefits than to ignore them or force them to go along because of senior management diktat.

The final stage to selling the business case is to prove that the project has delivered what was expected. There should be regular tracking of project progress, costs, and benefits achieved during and after the project. Benefits should be addressed in a post-project review report. The report should also be communicated to the ICT community and to the broader business community, to help others sell their business cases.

4 ORGANISATION, ROLES AND RESPONSIBILITIES

There are a number of strategic decisions concerning organisation and role assignments that must be made, actively or by default, in the process of implementing and running SAM. These decisions have major time and cost implications, and even greater implications for the benefits that can be achieved.

4.1 Decision about centralisation

One of the most important decisions that needs to be made for SAM is the degree of centralisation that will be implemented, and for which functions. This is a particularly critical decision for larger organisations with multiple divisions or business units that may have significant operational autonomy.

An analogy can be made with capital expenditure. It is possible for capital expenditure decision-making to be totally decentralised, but this is unusual, even in organisations that are otherwise highly decentralised. Many of the main benefits of SAM, as for capital expenditure, come from centralisation. These benefits include not only cost savings, but also Risk Management.

As at the time of writing this guide there have not been any formal studies to quantify the impact of centralisation on the benefits that SAM can bring. There are some ways in which decentralisation is superior. For example:

- Decentralisation allows for greater innovation and initiative in ICT (viewed by some as 'anarchy').

- It can be easier in a geographically decentralised organisation to demonstrate compliance to local authorities and regulators (although the overall cost will likely be higher than with a centralised approach).

- Some countries have requirements about the import/taxation of software that may not be easy to address within global purchasing arrangements.

However, there is considerable anecdotal evidence and logic to support the view that certain functions need to be centralised to produce the greatest possible benefits. (See Section 1.5 on the 'Benefits of SAM').

The functions that should be centralised go beyond SAM in the narrow sense, but SAM allows them to achieve their fullest potential. These functions include in particular:

- strategic ICT planning:
  - use of common ICT architectures
  - use of common products (standardisation)
  - rationalisation of software and hardware deployment
- strategic sourcing (software and hardware):
  - selection of resellers (possibly not based in HQ home country)
  - centrally negotiated pricing reflecting total purchasing power (especially important for software) and time-phased requirements (can be especially important for hardware)

- Risk Management:
  - legal compliance, including management of relationships with local authorities and compliance organisations
  - management of the impact of unexpected events on the organisation, e.g. licensing audits

- supply of software licensing expertise to the entire organisation

- coordination of reallocation of software and hardware resources between subsidiaries and business units, e.g. facilitating the redeployment of licences from units with excess, to those with growing needs.

Operational functions, however, may be handled on a more decentralised basis, including in particular:

- procurement processing

- deployment and installation

- operation and maintenance of the detailed SAM database including physical proof of licence (see Section 4.2).

Key message

The overall SAM processes need to strike a balance between 'globalisation' and 'localisation', with responsibilities distributed appropriately between the two.

4.2 Centralisation or decentralisation of SAM databases

Each organisation must decide how to implement its SAM database logically and physically. The decision has major time and cost implications.

In theory, the centralised functions described above would best be supported by a centralised SAM database. However, this may not be practical for a number of reasons:

- the parent company is a holding company that buys and sells subsidiaries frequently

- different subsidiaries or business units operate largely autonomously, and a centralised SAM database would require an unacceptable level of operational centralisation.

Nonetheless, it is still desirable to have a centralised SAM database to the extent consistent with operational requirements. The following approach is therefore recommended:

- The SAM database should be implemented as a physically-integrated centralised database to the extent practical. In principle, this should be at the level that corresponds to operational ICT responsibility, so that there would be a consolidated SAM database for each area of autonomous ICT responsibility. Responsibility for licensing compliance should also be clearly defined at this same level. Furthermore, physical proof of licence should be controlled at this level.

- Information from the separate detailed SAM databases must be provided to central functions on a regular and consistent basis to allow them to perform properly.

- Each SAM database may be a single physically integrated repository, or it may be a collection of freestanding but linked databases (a 'shared data environment') utilising the capabilities of different systems and tools. Full physical integration is desirable, but not easily achievable given the current state of the market for SAM and related tools.

See also Chapter 7 on 'Tools and Technology'.

4.3 Respective roles of Procurement Management and ICT Management

Another important decision to be made concerns the respective roles of Procurement Management and ICT Management. Responsibility for ICT procurement typically is defined in one of two ways:

- The department responsible for procurement (called 'Procurement', or 'Purchasing', or 'Supply Chain', etc.) has principal responsibility for managing all aspects of ICT procurement, with guidance to the extent necessary from ICT Management and personnel.
- The department responsible for ICT Management has principal responsibility for managing all aspects of ICT procurement, with guidance to the extent necessary from procurement personnel.

Some of the reasons for giving principal responsibility to the department responsible for procurement are:

- It is better placed to take cold economic decisions about the cost-justification of proposed expenditure, without being swayed by technology for its own sake.
- It is better prepared to deal with the legal paperwork of contracting.
- It has better negotiating skills, and can drive a harder bargain.
- It may have capacity to perform the work, compared to a possibly overworked ICT department.

Some of the reasons for giving principal responsibility to the ICT department are:

- ICT personnel have to live with the day-to-day consequences of procurement decisions, and will be more acutely focused on the operational implications of contracts, and what is necessary to meet contractual obligations.
- ICT personnel may also give more attention to other non-quantifiable factors, such as the quality of licensing advice provided by resellers.
- ICT personnel have a better view on strategic ICT directions and alternatives, which is where some of the most significant savings can be identified.
- ICT personnel may have more of a 'Risk-Management' orientation because of related ICT Risk Management concerns like security and data protection.

On balance, assuming these expected skill profiles, it is better to give the primary responsibility for ICT procurement to the ICT department, but with a strong supporting role being played by the procurement department. If strategic procurement functions are centralised as described in Section 4.1 above, then it will be easier to ensure sufficient qualified resources are dedicated to the job from both areas.

4.4   Roles and responsibilities

If SAM processes are to prove successful within an organisation, it is important that roles and responsibilities are clearly defined and agreed and that the scope of ownership of each of the processes is also defined and agreed. These roles and responsibilities should therefore be adapted to fit the individual requirements of each organisation in accordance with its size, nature, structure, culture and geographical distribution. In small organisations, one or two people will perform most of these roles.

4.4.1   Primary roles

- **Management sponsor:** It is important if SAM is to succeed within an organisation that sponsorship and commitment are obtained from senior managers both within the business and ICT. This will ensure that the visibility of SAM is maintained and that the organisational culture is developed to enable the SAM processes to succeed. It will enable sufficient budget and resources to be obtained. Management sponsorship and commitment must be maintained and not allowed to deteriorate.

- **Director with legal responsibility:** SAM implementations progress to a successful conclusion more rapidly when the support and commitment of the director with the legal responsibility for software assets is clearly identified. Once identified, he/she can usually be convinced of the benefits and need for SAM throughout the organisation.

- **Configuration Manager:** This is the person with overall responsibility for the configuration management process, as defined in ITIL terminology. This includes much of the scope of SAM. In an ITIL-compliant organisation, the individuals responsible for IT Asset Management and SAM might report to the Configuration Manager, although as defined in this guide it would mean an expansion of the role of Configuration Management.

- **IT Asset Manager:** This individual should be responsible for the management of all ICT assets within an organisation. He/she would have overall responsibility for establishing and maintaining the IT asset database. (This is technically part of the Configuration Management Database (CMDB) in ITIL terminology – see Chapter 9). This database should also contain all of the information required by SAM processes.

- **Software Asset Manager:** This is the person with responsibility for the management of all software assets within an organisation. This is a subset of the overall responsibility of the IT Asset Manager. It is essential if the responsibilities are separated that common processes and a common database are shared between the two roles. In some organisations, this role is often merged with that of the SAM Process Owner.

- **SAM Process Owner:** In some organisations, responsibility for the overall effectiveness and efficiency of SAM processes rests with the SAM Process Owner. This role is basically responsible for ensuring a continual process of improvement is applied to all SAM processes.

- **Asset Analysts or Configuration Librarians:** These are responsible for maintaining up-to-date (and historical) records of IT assets including software version control.

4.4.2   Complementary roles

■ **Auditors (internal and external):** Responsible for reviewing and auditing the SAM processes for efficiency, effectiveness and compliance.

■ **Procurement Management:** Responsible for all aspects of the procurement process within the end-user organisation.

■ **Legal Advice/Council:** Responsible for the provision of legal advice and guidance, contractual issues and legal matters.

■ **Change Manager:** Ensures that an effective Change Management process is in place to control all changes within the ICT infrastructure, including all changes to software.

■ **SAM Consultant:** Provides advice and guidance on all aspects of SAM best practice.

■ **Automation Analyst:** Responsible for the implementation, configuring and tailoring of tools to automate processes wherever it is cost-effective.

■ **Service Desk Manager:** Although this role is not strictly part of the SAM process, it is a vital one. The Service Desk Manager has a responsibility to ensure that all contacts with the Service Desk that uncover instances of unauthorised or unapproved software should be reported to the SAM exception processes as soon as possible for review and resolution.

■ **Security Manager:** This role is not strictly a part of the SAM processes but it has a crucial part to play. For example, the Security Manager should help ensure that all software is maintained at the recommended security 'patch level' so that security exposures from the use of software are minimised.

5 PROCESS OVERVIEW

The overall objective of all SAM processes is that of good corporate governance, namely:

> To manage, control and protect an organisation's software assets, including management of the risks arising from the use of those software assets.

This guide approaches SAM principally through a description of its processes, as do ITIL and BS 15000. An overview of the process areas for SAM is shown in Figure 5.1. These areas are similar to those for ITIL and BS 15000. The mappings of these processes to those of ITIL, BS 15000 and COBIT® (Control Objectives for Information and related Technology. Copyright 1996, 1998, 2000, The IT Governance Institute™) described in Chapter 9.

Overall Management Processes		
Overall management responsibility Risk assessment Policies and procedures	Competence, awareness and training Performance metrics and continuous improvement Service continuity and availability management	
Core Asset Management Processes		
Asset identification Asset control Status accounting	Database management Financial management	
Logistics Processes Requirements definition Design Evaluation Procurement Build Deployment Operation Optimisation Retirement	**Verification and Compliance Processes** Verification and audit Licensing compliance Security compliance Other compliance	**Relationship Processes** Contract management Supplier management Internal business relationship management Outsourcing management

Figure 5.1 – SAM process areas

This chapter gives:

- an overview of the objectives and constituent activities of each of the process areas of SAM
- detailed comments where appropriate about each of the process areas.

The comments given are limited to clarifying the scope of SAM processes, as there is already ample discussion in other ITIL publications and other professional materials about most other relevant generic areas, e.g. service continuity and Availability Management. More detail is given in this guide only where it is important for a proper understanding of SAM. The logistics processes in particular require the most detailed comments, with the greatest detail being given for the procurement process.

5.1 Overall management processes

The objective of the overall management processes is:

> To establish and maintain the management infrastructure within which the other SAM processes are implemented.

5.1.1 Overall management responsibility

Senior management has overall responsibility for all aspects of corporate governance. Increasingly, these responsibilities are being codified in different Corporate Governance standards, such as Turnbull in the UK and Sarbanes-Oxley in the US. The overall responsibility for SAM should be explicitly linked into these standards to the extent possible.

As part of this issue, it is critical to ensure that responsibility for SAM is clearly defined within the remit of specific positions. While this may be simple in principle, in practice it is often not done, with the result that nobody really takes responsibility. For example, a board of directors may consider its group head of ICT to have overall responsibility for SAM, including compliance issues. However, in practice this individual may not have the remit or authority to ensure appropriate systems for SAM throughout the organisation. This is typically a problem in organisations with decentralised management structures but a central ICT unit providing some, but not all, ICT services.

5.1.2 Risk assessment

Management is responsible for making and regularly updating assessments of risks to which the organisation is exposed. Ultimately, these assessments are the drivers for most of the other control actions taken by the organisation, including SAM. The major risk areas for SAM are listed in Section 1.5.

5.1.3 Policies and procedures

Management is responsible for ensuring that appropriate policies and procedures are put in place to achieve appropriate SAM throughout the organisation. Most important is a clear central statement of SAM policy, which is effectively communicated throughout the organisation with mechanisms to ensure periodic employee acknowledgement. An example of such a policy statement is included in Appendix G. The mechanisms used to promulgate such policies will typically be used to promulgate other critical corporate policies, such as on information confidentiality and security measures.

5.1.4 Competence, awareness and training

Management needs to ensure that relevant personnel have appropriate levels of competence. For example, licensing is a complex area, and it requires a reasonable level of competence to manage correctly. Normally it is desirable to have this competence in-house. It may be possible to rely on a commercial partner (e.g. a reseller) to provide much assistance in this area, but ultimately the responsibility for compliance is with the organisation itself, and not with the reseller. This knowledge of licensing issues must be kept up to date as the terms and conditions of software usage frequently change.

All employees should also typically have a level of general awareness of SAM and licensing requirements. Some volume licensing agreements make such awareness efforts a contractual requirement. This awareness can be achieved via the same mechanisms as are used to communicate policies to employees.

5.1.5 Performance metrics and continuous improvement

The overall management processes include responsibility for Performance Management of the SAM processes, including:

- definition of measurements, metrics and KPIs
- performance monitoring, reporting and reviewing
- continuous process improvement (Plan–Do–Check–Act).

5.1.6 IT Service Continuity Management and Availability Management

The overall management processes include responsibility for IT Service Continuity Management and Availability Management related to SAM. This responsibility includes ensuring:

- that the SAM database is backed up and protected by appropriate availability and contingency measures
- that there is reasonable security for all assets and all proofs of licence, with adequate backup records in case of events such as fire
- that the organisation's contingency provisions are themselves subject to proper SAM, e.g. that hot backup systems are properly licensed.

Key message

Licensing assets including proof of licence need to be properly stored and protected. Loss of these assets may require replacement through repurchase. In some cases, these licences may no longer be available for sale. If they are available, there might be new terms and conditions that could even affect the original installation. Proper care of licensing assets avoids all of these issues.

5.2 Core Asset Management processes

The objective of core Asset Management processes is:

To identify and to maintain information about software assets throughout their lifecycle, and to manage physical assets related to software.

Traditionally, Asset Management has been seen as the maintenance of an asset register and a set of processes for managing the financial aspects of purchasing, depreciation and retirement of an organisation's assets. However, it is actually much broader than this.

5.2.1   Asset identification

Each organisation needs to define which asset items it needs to control as part of its SAM system, and what attributes it needs for each asset. A distinction should be made between the items to be controlled, and the inventory system for those items. The asset items that normally need to be controlled are:

- a secure software library of master copies and media, together with controlled distributed copies
- licences purchased
- contractual documentation (agreements, licence terms and conditions, etc.)
- other proof of licence (licence confirmations, etc.)
- installed software
- standard configuration definitions/instances (with base-lining as planned, as released and as installed with fixes/updates)
- financial data (for management and financial accounting and for tax purposes).

See Appendix D for suggestions about the contents of a SAM database.

5.2.2   Asset control

Asset control ensures that assets are controlled and authorised through their lifecycle. It is closely linked to some of the logistics processes.

5.2.3   Status accounting

Status accounting provides an audit trail of changes in the status of assets through the stages of the lifecycle.

5.2.4   Database management

Database management as defined in this guide is focused on the purely technical and housekeeping aspects of the SAM database. It consists of:

- database design and optimisation
- all relevant housekeeping activities on the SAM database.

5.2.5   Financial Management

Financial Management is one of the core processes within SAM. For any organisation, relevant cost information should be captured, not just for software assets themselves, but also for related processes, to help justify SAM finances and budgets and overall process improvements. SAM Financial Management includes:

- ensuring the preparation of reliable financial information for all software assets, including during their procurement, operation (e.g. regular depreciation) and subsequent retirement and disposal

- the collection of cost/benefit information related to the use of software assets, to allow the calculation of TCO and ROI
- proper consideration of accounting and tax treatments.

Relevant expertise should be used to ensure that accounting and tax treatments for software assets are appropriate and tax efficient. Depending on the country involved and other factors such as tax position and industry, significant tax savings may be possible through a combination of good record-keeping and proper application of the relevant tax regulations.

5.3 Logistics processes

The objective of logistics processes is:

> To control all activities affecting the progress of software through its lifecycle.

The logistics processes of SAM map to the stages of the application lifecycle. The application lifecycle from the Applications Management module of the IT Infrastructure Library (ITIL) principally refers to the more limited lifecycle for in-house developed software:

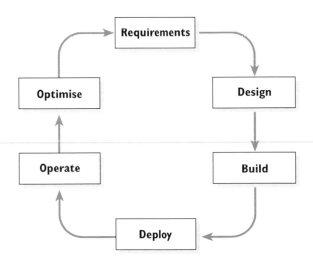

Figure 5.2 – The application lifecycle from ITIL Applications Management

This lifecycle has been extended for this guide to encompass the additional stages required for externally sourced software. The SAM logistics processes are the same as the processes in this modified application lifecycle.

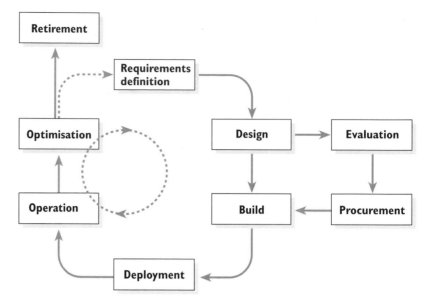

Figure 5.3 – The modified application lifecycle (including externally sourced software)

The logistics processes may need to be applied at any level of activity from highly extensive to the relatively minor:

- A major ICT project based on a new architecture and infrastructure will dictate extensive attention to all of the lifecycle steps.

- An end-user on-line request for the automated installation of a new application (from a list of pre-approved alternatives) using pull technology will also be covered by the application lifecycle, within the context of pre-established blanket approvals.

SAM logistical processes enable the right software to be delivered to the right locations with the right quality and within the right timescale. The trigger for the commencement of logistics activity should be the initiation of a change within the Change Management process, as defined in ITIL terminology. This trigger event could be a major corporate reassessment of ICT strategy; a software manufacturer announcement of product obsolescence; an individual ICT project proposal; or a request by an individual user for the installation of a new application. However major or minor, the process requirements as defined in this section should apply to all such situations, with a corresponding degree of complexity or simplicity in the application of these requirements.

5.3.1 Requirements definition

The initial stage of any software product involves the requirements-gathering and definition stage. This is the most important stage of the lifecycle and is where the business needs are identified and documented with regard to any new requirements. Information and data obtained from the SAM processes and tools are often essential to these requirements-gathering activities.

These requirements should include all aspects of the software including the functional requirements, the non-functional requirements and the usability requirements. It should also incorporate all of the intended service targets for the 'operate stage' of the lifecycle within a Service Level Requirement (SLR) document.

The functional requirements are those specifically required to support a business process. Non-functional requirements address the operational and management needs. The principal involvement of SAM within this stage is to ensure that all of the needs of SAM within the subsequent stages of the software lifecycle are included within the overall set of requirements.

Once the requirements have been agreed and documented then business cases, feasibility studies and cost-benefit analyses should be completed. The project should only progress to subsequent stages of the lifecycle if the results of these analyses indicate appropriate business benefits will be realised.

Another issue that may need to be considered within a requirements exercise is upgrading software. The upgrade of software also needs to consider:

- Do we need a new release, version or patch level of the software? (e.g. increased required functionality)
- What are the business benefits deriving from its usage? (e.g. increased business productivity or improved product performance)
- What are the risks associated with continuing with the existing release, version or patch level? (e.g. manufacturer has withdrawn support of the existing product.)

5.3.2 Design

Design for in-house developed software includes the design of the application itself together with the design of the environment or operational model within which the application has to run. For externally sourced software, often 'blueprint' operational models are built and tested to ensure conformance to functional requirements, and consistency and integration with other systems within the organisation.

Consideration should be given to the applications architecture, systems architecture and the management architecture within the overall design, to ensure that any development or 'blueprint' operational models are consistent with the overall organisational strategies and policies.

5.3.3 Evaluation

The evaluation stage is primarily for externally sourced software although some aspects may be appropriate where in-house applications are being designed and developed. Formal Terms of Reference (ToR) and Statement of Requirements (SoR) documents may be produced and circulated to prospective suppliers. Evaluation criteria and processes are also documented for the assessment of alternative proposals and may also be circulated to prospective suppliers. The proposal that 'best fits' the evaluation criteria should be selected for implementation.

This stage may also include aspects of design and design evaluation, although principally the design will be part of overall Information Systems (IS) and Information and Communications Technologies (ICT) strategies. All of the ongoing operational needs of SAM should be considered and evaluated at this point and must be met by the selected solution.

This stage will include the selection of the most cost-effective software licensing agreements.

5.3.4 Procurement

This stage of the lifecycle is primarily for externally sourced software and is entered once the evaluation process has been completed and the most appropriate solution has been selected. It may also be necessary to complete some of the activities within this stage for in-house developed software if hardware or additional software is required, e.g. development software or run-time licences for production software.

Even though SAM is actively involved in the previous logistics stages, with procurement the need for good SAM becomes especially critical. If appropriate procurement processes are not followed correctly and consistently, then problems will be created that will be costly and difficult to detect and subsequently correct.

The sub-processes of SAM procurement are illustrated in Figure 5.4. The flow through the sub-processes is dependent upon whether distribution copies and sufficient licences are already available for use within the organisation, and upon contractual requirements for when licences must be ordered (e.g. before installing, monthly after installing, or yearly after installing). More detailed comments are also given about some of the detailed sub-processes.

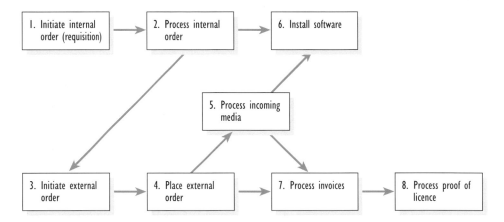

Figure 5.4 – The SAM procurement process

Process internal order

During the processing of the internal order, a check should be made as to whether there are already any available licences free to be used. These may be available, for example, because there was a bulk purchase which has not all been used up, or because licences are free because of retirement or rationalisation of deployment elsewhere. A centralised view of licence availability gives the best cost-saving opportunity, especially for large organisations with many units operating largely autonomously. (There also need to be corresponding procedures to formally transfer the licences if management is handled on a decentralised basis.)

Initiate external order

A consistent finding in many organisations is that there is poor coordination of purchasing arrangements, with the result that purchases are often made that do not take advantage of the best available alternatives. For example, a business unit may purchase a product locally at retail prices rather than through a centralised and more cost-effective contract. The process for initiating the external order should ensure that the most appropriate source is chosen for fulfilling the order.

Process proof of licence

There are two major cases to consider for processing proof of licence, and each has a major issue associated with it:

- **Non-volume and OEM proof of licence:** These licences do not name the licensee. The main concern is to ensure the product's authenticity, i.e. that it is not counterfeit.

- **Volume proof of licence:** These name the licensee. The main concern is to ensure that the required documentation from the software manufacturer in the customer's name is actually received.

Each of these is dealt with briefly below.

- **Ensuring product authenticity:** There is a serious risk of organisations purchasing counterfeit software through non-volume licensing channels. In part this is because of the attractiveness of this market to counterfeiters, and in part, it is due to the limited attention often paid to product authenticity by end-user organisations, and sometimes even by resellers and distributors. The organisation should make reasonable checks for the authenticity of the software it is purchasing, especially when risk factors for counterfeiting are elevated. See Section B.4 for a discussion of counterfeiting, and what an organisation should do about it.

The biggest 'red flag' for counterfeit software is low price.

If one reseller charges significantly less than another reseller for the same quantity of the same product, beware of counterfeits. Explanations of 'grey imports' or 'clearance stock' are likely to be deceptions.

Ensure that you get a breakdown of hardware and software costs for any package deals offered.

- **Ensuring receipt of volume proof of licence:** Another important issue in the procurement process is checking for the receipt of the volume proof of licence. This is complicated by the fact that many volume-licensing situations involve a tri-partite relationship, with the order going to a reseller, but with the licence confirmation coming back from the software manufacturer. It is possible to insist on receiving the licence confirmation before payment, similar to situations involving physical delivery of goods. However, this will often be problematical because of the impact it will have on reseller cashflow. As a result, an alternative procedure can be used, as indicated in Figure 5.5.

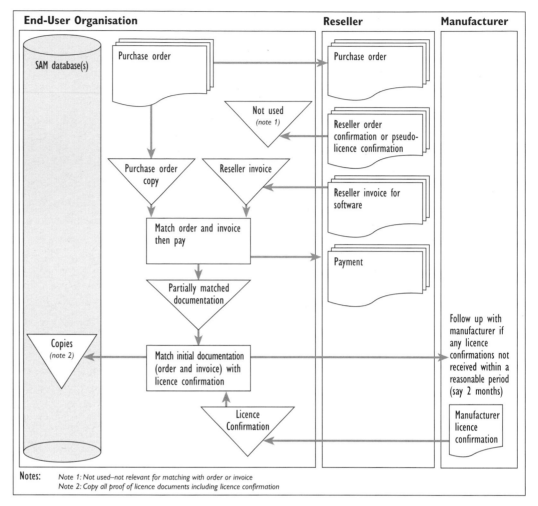

Figure 5.5 – Checking receipt of manufacturer proof of licence

The licence confirmation may be physical or electronic. Note that if the software manufacturer licence confirmation is not received directly from the software manufacturer, it should also be checked for authenticity. There have been cases of counterfeit volume licensing confirmations.

5.3.5 Build

The build stage is extensively used with in-house developed software, but is also relevant for creating new builds of externally sourced software. For in-house developed software, it encompasses the development, coding, integration, building and testing of all of the components within the new release. This should involve the use of separate development, build and test environments. All of these environments should mirror the proposed live environments as closely as possible. Once these build and test activities have been completed, then the approved release can be deployed throughout the organisation.

For externally sourced software, this stage consists of integration, building and extensive testing. Once complete the approved release can be deployed throughout the organisation.

This process will ensure that only correct versions of software that are 'fit for purpose' will be released to the organisation minimising the disruption often caused by problems with new releases. Often pilot tests are completed prior to full deployment to minimise the risk and disruption to the business and accomplish this release in a controlled manner. In some organisations, a staging environment is used to rigorously test new releases before distribution to the live environment. The ongoing requirements of the SAM processes should also be built and tested within each of these environments, e.g. the ability of discovery tools to identify properly the new software or versions.

SAM should help ensure that the release consists only of those components that are approved for release and that all components are authentic, licensed, supported and legal. SAM should also ensure that all of the proposed destination environments have the necessary contracts and licences.

5.3.6 Deployment

During the deployment stage, all components of a release are deployed to their agreed and approved destination environments. SAM is responsible for monitoring the deployment process so that software is only deployed to the environment for which licences and contracts have been obtained. It is essential that during this process the details contained within the SAM database are updated to reflect the progress of the deployment project in a timely fashion. This is the stage where the most non-compliances can be introduced with regard to the use of unlicensed software within an organisation.

The deployment mechanisms used may vary significantly depending on the extensiveness of the deployment required. Physical deployment may be required, especially if new hardware is also involved. Push technologies are useful for mass deployments to machines determined by ICT, including for security patches and anti-virus updates. Pull technologies are especially useful for deployment to individuals requesting specific applications where approval can be automated or where there is pre-approval. These are areas of considerable focus by ICT departments independent of any formal focus on SAM. However, the deployment process needs to be integrated into SAM to ensure that all deployments are properly authorised, including having licences, and that the SAM database is properly updated as a result.

There is one important licensing 'exception condition' that deployment functionality must be able to handle. This is deployment of software to machines that are already properly licensed, e.g. where software must be reinstalled because of hardware failure or major software problems, but there is no need to purchase additional licences. The exposure here is that this procedural loophole could be abused to install additional unauthorised software. Procedures should ensure that reinstallations are supported by checking for proper prior authorisations just as for new installations.

Another issue that must be addressed during deployment is the handling of licensing terms and conditions that frequently must be accepted during the installation of software, both commercial and non-commercial. Such terms may even authorise the installation of 'spy-ware' and other unintended functionality. If software has been properly tested before deployment, this issue will already have been addressed. The main concern lies with employees who may be able to install software independently.

5.3.7 Operation

This stage of the lifecycle is responsible for monitoring exceptions in ongoing operations relevant to SAM. There are two major aspects to this activity:

- Ensuring that the ICT services are operated, supported and managed according to the service targets agreed within the original SLR, which should now evolve into Service Level Agreements (SLAs) for the operational services. Example targets would be deployment time for security patches, and workstation overhead for running metering tools.

■ Identifying individual exceptions to SAM policies, e.g. identifying instances of unauthorised software installed on workstations immediately or soon after installation.

There is overlap between these requirements, and the requirements of the two other areas, with the differentiator being whether exceptions are identified on an immediate basis or on a periodic basis. These areas are:

■ Compliance processes – see Section 5.4

■ Performance metrics and continuous improvement – see Paragraph 5.1.5.

5.3.8   Optimisation

Optimisation is a process that overlaps with general management processes, with the objective being to ensure continuous improvement. This focus on improvement can operate in several areas:

■ **Software deployment optimisation:** Active software usage (as opposed to just installation or availability) should be reviewed periodically to determine whether deployment corresponds to end-user needs. It may also be appropriate to conduct end-user surveys of what software is considered necessary. A common finding is that there may be significant levels of software deployed that are not being actively used. Depending on licensing terms and conditions, it may be possible to redeploy these unnecessary licences to other users or locations where they are needed. While the savings may be limited initially, as purchased licences generally cannot be returned, future savings may be achieved by avoiding future additional purchases for other users.

■ **Performance targets:** Service performance achievements, targets, usage and fit-for-purpose levels should be continuously monitored and wherever they are threatened or breached, action should be initiated to prevent future such occurrences. This will necessitate a continuous improvement process within the operational and optimisation stages of the lifecycle as indicated in Figure 5.3. Some of the actions may also drive more major processes, e.g. the development of new systems capabilities to achieve required improvements.

■ **Overall efficiency and effectiveness:** It should also be an integral aspect of this part of the software lifecycle to continually asses the SAM processes for efficiency and effectiveness and to feed back suggested improvements whenever possible. This should include reviews for optimisation and supportability with partners and suppliers (e.g. when a supplier may stop supporting a version for reason of age, or when licence conditions are changed or should be changed).

5.3.9   Retirement

The final stage of the lifecycle is the retirement phase. (This is sometimes referred to as the 'write-off' phase, but write-offs may happen before retirement for tax efficiency purposes or because of long asset life. Therefore, retirement is not the same as write-off, even though they may often happen together.) Retirement occurs when services and systems cease to be functional or available for any reason, or are no longer cost-effective to use. Once it is decided to retire a software asset, it needs to be dealt with appropriately. Often software remains within the operational environment, but is not subject to patches, upgrades, support, etc. This can cause licensing and communications issues and needs to be managed with the software progressed into retirement. Software retirement has many potential issues to consider:

- **Hardware retirement:** Software retirement is often associated with the retirement of hardware, and needs to be dealt with appropriately:
  - OEM software: Normally, OEM software that was supplied with hardware can only be used with that hardware, so it cannot be 'recycled'. However, the relevant proof of OEM licences will normally make the equipment more valuable on the secondary market, so these original materials can be disposed of together with the hardware (if they have been properly stored, and are accessible.)
  - Non-OEM software. Often, the licences for non-OEM software (including upgrades previously applied to OEM software) are transferable to other hardware. In these cases, the installed version cannot be left on the hardware when it is disposed of. In any case, it is normally desirable to wipe hard disks to remove confidential data, which will also have the effect of removing the software. If the licences being moved are upgrades which were originally applied to OEM licenses, it will be necessary to have another properly qualified underlying licence for any machine to which it is transferred.

- **Retirement of deployment, but not of licences:**
  - Sometimes a version of software will be retired, or even a complete product, so there will be no more installations of the specific software. However, the licences themselves will not be retired, but rather provide a basis for upgrade licences. In these cases, the installed versions of the software will need to be uninstalled, but the licences will need to be retained and linked to the new licences which will be based on them.

- **Options for recycling:** Where software and licences are both being retired, it may be possible to consider recycling alternatives, depending on detailed licensing terms and conditions:

  Transfer/sale to related organisations: Licensing terms and conditions, including under volume licensing contracts, often allow for transfer of licences to related companies, perhaps with specific procedural and notification requirements.
  - Transfer/sale to unrelated organisations: Non-volume licensing terms and conditions (including retail and OEM) often allow for transfer of licences to anyone, subject to full transfer of all relevant materials. Volume licensing contracts may also allow this, but more often require the formal consent of the software manufacturer. There is no guarantee of success, but if the amounts involved are significant, and there is a realistic market, then it is probably worth checking with the manufacturer.

- **Archiving:** It is good practice to archive a copy of all retired software. One reason for this is that it might be necessary at some future date to restore retired software to be able to access historical data, for example to meet statutory requirements for access to information supporting the financial statements or tax returns. There might be licensing implications for such archiving, and these should be investigated. Contractual conditions might be negotiated initially to ensure that such future needs are covered.

5.4 Verification and compliance processes

The objective of compliance processes is:

> To detect, escalate and manage all exceptions to SAM policies, processes, procedures and licence use rights.

Figure 5.6 illustrates how the compliance processes relate to the SAM database and to real-world instances.

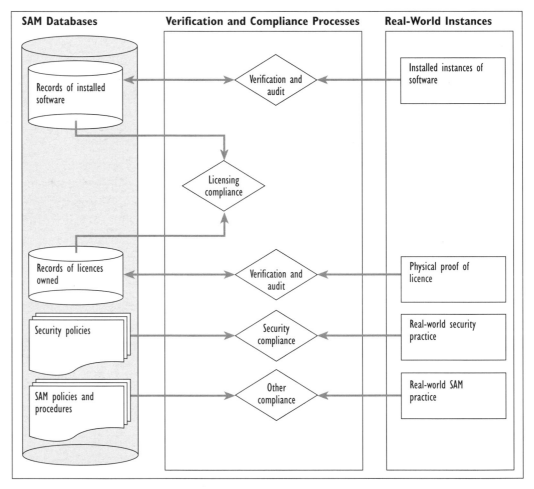

Figure 5.6 – SAM verification and compliance processes

Compliance processes must include sub-processes for identifying and resolving SAM exception conditions and non-compliances.

No matter how comprehensive and extensive the SAM processes are there will always be some areas of non-compliance. Any truly effective SAM processes will have automated methods for trapping these non-compliances and escalating them to the appropriate resources for immediate attention. The SAM processes should not only be capable of trapping and escalating non-compliances but should also instigate remedial action to processes and procedures wherever possible to prevent recurrences.

5.4.1 Verification and audit

The objective of the verification and audit process is to ensure that the SAM records accurately reflect what is actually held, and that appropriate corrective actions are undertaken when discrepancies are identified. There are two main issues to address:

- whether asset counts and related information are accurate
- whether the underlying assets – especially licences – are genuine, i.e. not counterfeit.

Accurate records

The process for verifying the integrity of records of software actually in use is one of the most fully developed in the market. In particular, there are a large number of software 'discovery' tools that help to identify software in use. Further information about these tools is given in Chapter 7.

In spite of the comparatively advanced state of this type of tool, there are still major restrictions that need to be noted:

- Available discovery tools are best at identifying major commercial products. They tend to be weak at identifying the following types of products which generally require extensive work to identify adequately:
  - in-house developed products, including identification of versions and patches applied
  - software which end-users are particularly liable to install without proper authorisation, such as file-swapping software, and instant messaging programs.
- Available discovery tools are often limited in the platforms on which they can be used. This is an issue not just for different types of workstation machines, but also for PDAs, SmartPhones, and other mobile devices.
- Discovery tools are strongest in networked environments. There will always be complications of using discovery tools for non-networked machines, e.g. for free-standing dedicated uses, or for mobile machines rarely connected.

Verifying the integrity of records of licences held is a manually intensive activity. The main work should be performed when the records are initially created, but there should also be periodic or continuous processes to confirm the continuing accuracy and completeness of records held. One of the main issues to be addressed as part of this process is verifying the authenticity of proof of licences, considered in the next section.

Verification of authenticity of licences:

There is a small but very real risk of organisations purchasing counterfeit licences, especially if they purchase through 'grey' import channels. These problems occur not only for small businesses, buying from bargain sources, but also for major organisations, both governmental and commercial. The risks to the company are, at the very least, those of not having any licences at all. Depending on the circumstances, local legislation and enforcement, they could be much worse.

Licence authenticity should initially be checked as part of the original procurement process, as described in Paragraph 5.3.4. There may also be a periodic review of the authenticity of existing licences following the same principles as described in that section.

5.4.2 Licensing compliance

Licensing compliance processes are responsible for ensuring that the use of all software within the organisation remains within all legal and contractual terms and conditions. Licensing compliance consists of:

- The identification, alerting, capture and resolution of all exception conditions and non-conformances relating to the use of unlicensed software. These should include:
  - the identification and review of all changes in software within the organisation, ensuring that they are within current licensing agreements
  - the interception of any SAM abnormalities recorded by the Service Desk or Incident Management
  - the interception and detection of any unapproved software purchases
  - escalation or feedback mechanisms for the instigation of reactive and remedial actions, relating to software licensing.

- The correction and prevention of licensing shortfalls and the identification and highlighting of software overuse and redundancy situations.

5.4.3 Security compliance

A compliance programme should address compliance with security policies and standards and should include:

- ensuring that software policies are consistent with security policies and plans
- ensuring all security patches are being applied promptly to all relevant machines.

5.4.4 Other compliance (e.g. with other policies and procedures)

A compliance programme should address compliance with all other significant policies and procedures, including the overall SAM policies and procedures. It should ensure that:

- SAM polices are consistent with all other corporate policies and strategies
- the impact of non-compliance (to the organisation and to the individual, e.g. loss of job) is well communicated to all employees
- the implementation of all cost-justifiable preventative mechanisms such as for the prevention of unauthorised software downloads from the Internet and the inhibiting of certain attachment file types on e-mails.

5.5 Relationship Management processes

The objective of Relationship Management processes is:

> To manage all relationships within the business, and with partners and suppliers, to agreed contractual, legal and documented service terms and targets.

Both internal and external relationships need to be managed. External relationships that need to be managed include those with software manufacturers and their resellers, and also any outsourcers who are providing related services internally. Internal relationships that need to be managed include those with both management and end-users.

External partners (software manufacturers, resellers, outsourcers, etc.) may be sources of significant information. For example, they may be able to provide records of licences purchased as a check on, or possibly in place of, internal records, which may be incomplete. The main role of this process is:

- the overall coordination and management of all contracts and licence agreements with all software suppliers and resellers
- the overall coordination and management of all relationships with the customers and the business.

5.5.1 Contract Management

Contract Management is a specialised aspect of external Partner Management, which deserves separate discussion. Contract Management includes:

- the review, negotiation and management of all software contracts including the structuring of software contracts
- the monitoring of supplier performance to ensure suppliers meet or exceed their contracted service levels.

Proper contract structuring is an important aspect of SAM. Where possible, contracts should be structured to reflect the lines of responsibility for SAM. For example, in a decentralised organisation, it will typically facilitate Licence Management if each separate unit managing its own software has its own sub-agreement for reporting purposes. The alternative (centralised reporting) can make it difficult to reconcile orders to licence confirmations, to identify licences at the time of demergers and, in general, to manage licences at the level where SAM responsibility lies.

Software 'maintenance' or 'insurance' contracts need to be monitored against software releases, to ensure all available upgrade rights are identified, even if not immediately utilised.

5.5.2 Supplier Management

Supplier Management includes the management of relationships with all software suppliers, resellers, partners and software manufacturers including regular review meetings and the agreement of contract or SLA performance measurements, metrics and KPIs. This is principally to ensure that contract expectations are clearly set out and understood, all software is purchased from reputable sources and that the suppliers, resellers, partners and software manufacturers are reputable, have a long-term future and are providing value for money.

5.5.3 Internal Business Relationship Management

Internal Business Relationship Management (BRM) includes the management of the relationship with internal business managers on all aspects related to software and its use within the organisation. This may be done directly with the business managers or may be through a centralised point of contact within the ICT organisation such as the Service Level Manager, an Account Manager or Business Relationship Manager.

It also includes the provision of adequate training and education on the relevant SAM aspects for customers and users of software, ensuring recognition of the software policy and its use.

5.5.4 Outsourcing

Outsourcing is a special case of managing an external supplier who performs a role, function or process typically kept in-house. The range of such situations includes:

- **basic:** roll-outs, or ongoing technical support
- **intermediate:** procurement, etc.
- **extensive:** turn-key, outsourcing agreements, managed services, etc. e.g. for Asset Management.

Most of the comments already made about both internal and external relationships apply. Additional issues, which need to be considered, include:

- conflicts of interest regarding sharing of asset information, especially with multiple outsourcers
- possible negative effects of compensation criteria (e.g. an outsourcer may be paid based on the number of hardware devices managed, with the result that hardware savings will probably not be in the outsourcer's best interest)
- need to clarify who has ownership of licences
- termination implications, e.g. transfer of licence ownership.

There is also a potential issue when an outsourcer is responsible for installing software, whether as part of a major roll-out, or for one-off installations of software by technical support personnel. There is a significant risk that the responsibility for licences will not be clearly defined, with the result that each side thinks the other is responsible for obtaining software licences. The risk is ultimately with the end-user organisation, so it should be clearly stated contractually if the outsourcer is to provide the licences and what the terms of ownership and maintenance will be. There should be appropriate follow-up to ensure that the relevant proof of licence is obtained.

5.6 Special situations

Several special situations may create risk that needs to be managed.

5.6.1 Mergers/demergers and reorganisations

SAM, and licensing in particular, is often overlooked as part of mergers and demergers. Proper 'due diligence' at these times should ensure that SAM is understood, including licence ownership and novation. If this is not done, the acquiring company may be acquiring an unexpected financial and legal exposure due to inadequate licensing. Or a demerged company may subsequently find itself without adequate software licences.

There may be special procedural or documentation requirements for such situations, which must be determined by reference to contractual documentation or software manufacturers. There may also be some limitations as to the transferability of some licences, e.g. the non-divisibility of some volume licences. There are also times when divesting or merger firms require special 'rights to use' agreements with software manufacturers/suppliers.

Similar considerations may apply to internal reorganisations, especially if they affect the organisation, geographic location or responsibility for ICT assets. As discussed in Section 4.2, it is recommended that licensing documentation is held at the same place as the operational responsibility for licensing compliance.

5.6.2   Downsizing

Downsizing will normally result in inventories of unused licences that may be redeployed elsewhere in the organisation or potentially sold to third parties. It is recommended that these issues should be discussed with the software manufacturers first if the intention is to sell the licences to third parties.

One difficult issue to address is how to deal with downsizing of an organisation that was not originally fully licensed. Legally, the obligation to purchase licences was incurred when software was initially used, and did not disappear when usage ceased.

5.6.3   Novation (customer/reseller/manufacturer legal changes)

The requirement for novation may arise when an organisation reforms itself and wishes to transfer all of its existing contracts and assets to the new organisation. This situation occurs, for example, within central and local government organisations, when departments, agencies and complete organisations are restructured. It is necessary in these situations that all suppliers and resellers are contacted to inform them that all of the assets and contracts have novated across to the new organisation.

Novation is not an automatic right, and it may be desirable to consider this right during original contract negotiations. The supplier (and sometimes the customer) may use the occasion of novation to insist on renegotiating the contract, including changes to the terms and conditions, volume discount, the actual price, and the rights that the purchaser has (i.e. they may not be able to use it in the same way or the same people may not be able to use as before).

6 IMPLEMENTATION OVERVIEW

The most difficult aspect of any process is its initial implementation. This has to be achieved while maintaining normal 'business as usual' processes and workloads. The implementation of SAM processes is no different, and can be broken down into four distinct stages:

- preparation
- getting there
- staying there
- proving that you are staying there.

One person should be appointed to own all of these stages and to run the initial project of establishing efficient SAM processes. Ideally, this same person should also own and be accountable for all of the ongoing and improvement aspects of the SAM processes. Where possible, processes already in existence within the organisation should be used or adapted to fit the required SAM solution. It should be emphasised that a programme of evaluation and assessment should be undertaken by the organisation to identify effective processes and build on them as appropriate.

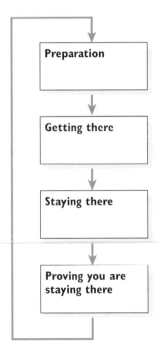

Figure 6.1 – SAM implementation

6.1 Preparation

Adequate preparation is always a critical success factor for any implementation. As a minimum, this stage should consist of the following elements:

- Reviewing the current situation with regard to the existing level of the management of software assets.
- Scoping and sizing the task, developing an outline project plan of the stages,

timescales, activities, costs and risks associated with the implementation of SAM. This would involve:

- conducting sample surveys to determine the size and nature of the challenge for implementing SAM. This should include all aspects of the ICT infrastructure including server systems, network systems, as well as PCs, PDAs, etc.
- ultimately, this will require as a minimum the development and maintenance of a complete hardware and software inventory database. This is the basis of any set of SAM processes.

■ Defining a vision and a desired state for the implementation of SAM within the organisation, including objectives, deliverables, measurements, metrics, Key Performance Indicators (KPIs) and Critical Success Factors (CSFs). All of these should be defined for the overall SAM process and for each of the constituent processes.

■ Agreeing and appointing ownership and responsibility for the SAM processes and their implementation. There may be different people responsible for the ownership of SAM processes during the implementation project and the subsequent ongoing operation of the processes.

■ Identifying and assessing software risks and creating a risk register.

■ Producing a business case justifying the approach to SAM within the organisation (see Chapter 3).

■ Obtaining sign-off, commitment and sponsorship for the project from both the business and IT, including the commitment of the necessary budget and resources for the successful implementation of the project.

■ Preventing a worsening situation, by identifying 'stopgap' processes to prevent greater use of uncontrolled software within the organisation.

■ Highlighting any problems and raising the profile of continued non-conformance.

■ Raising the awareness of the situation within both the business and IT, producing communication, education and training plans for all areas of the organisation.

■ Identifying 'quick wins' to help obtain buy-in to the project.

■ Producing and agreeing an implementation project plan together with agreed budgets, resources and responsibilities, including the identification of associated issues and risks together with all cost-effective mitigation actions.

■ Designing the overall SAM process and scoping all of the constituent processes, as detailed in Chapter 5.

■ Reviewing the SAM tools and database(s) for the comprehensiveness of their content and solution in underpinning the roles and processes.

How do you know when you are prepared? Consider the following questions.

- Has sponsorship for the SAM project been committed to at a senior management or board level?

- Has the profile of SAM been raised within the organisation and is the SAM culture developing?

- Have the vision and strategy for SAM been documented and agreed?

- Has the business case been accepted and approved?

- Have the budget and resources been committed to and are they available?

- Has a detailed plan been produced and accepted?

6.2 Getting there

The second stage consists of implementing the agreed project plan ensuring that the project meets all of its proposed targets:

- Managing and implementing the agreed plan.

- Developing an overall software policy encompassing all aspects of software and its use within the organisation (see Appendix G).

- Accepting and agreeing to the overall policy by senior management within the business and ICT and the commitment and support to its implementation in all areas of the organisation.

- Distributing, publicising, communicating, implementing and enforcing the software policy throughout the organisation. It is essential that the policy is universally accepted and implemented in all areas of the organisation as a company standard.

- Developing a corporate culture within the organisation in which all personnel understand the difference between the use of approved and unapproved software.

- Reviewing the risk register and the implementation of software risk mitigation actions using cost-justifiable countermeasures.

- Designing, developing and implementing an accurate and comprehensive set of SAM databases.

- Creating a 'ring-fenced' store of the master media of all approved, operational software in use within the organisation. The storage details of all media should be recorded within the SAM database, including details of the original supplier of the software and format of the data. A detailed record of any software media taken from the store of master media should be kept, signing in and out the media with reasons for its use and a signature by the individual taking it. The master software media should be kept under lock and key at all times, possibly in a safe to minimise associated risks.

- Creating a repository for the protection and retention of all software contracts, authenticity certificates and licence agreements. The storage details of all documents should be recorded within the SAM database.

- Creating and obtaining agreement for the detailed design documentation of all of the

SAM processes, including process deliverables, interfaces, dependencies, measurements, metrics, KPIs and CSFs. The SAM processes should encompass all of the process areas contained within Chapter 5.

■ Implementing the agreed SAM processes, together with process roles and responsibilities. This stage of the project may also involve the deployment and implementation of additional tools to facilitate the automation of the SAM processes wherever possible. This could be achieved using a 'big bang' deployment of the tools and processes but is much more likely to use some form of phased deployment throughout the organisation (see Chapter 7).

■ Managing roll-out of training and awareness of tools and processes.

■ Collecting and analysing all of the information on software assets and their usage.

■ Reviewing software purchasing processes to ensure the best licensing terms, contracts and prices for software acquisition and that all software is authentically purchased and properly registered both internally and externally with the software suppliers.

■ Preparing project progress reports and reviews.

■ Monitoring and reviewing all objectives, measurements, metrics, KPIs, and CSFs to ensure that the project has successfully met with all of its planned targets. This is the action that ensures you reach the 'desired state'.

■ Selecting, testing and deploying new or updated SAM tools.

■ Defining and agreeing on report content, structure, frequency and distribution.

■ Conducting an end-of-project review and sign-off for each part of the overall iterative process. The lessons learnt can then be fed into the next project.

How do you know when you have got there? Consider the following questions.

■ Have all the implementation objectives been met?

■ Have all the project deliverables been signed off?

■ Have all of the business benefits been realised?

■ Have all the CSFs been achieved?

■ Has the 'desired state' been achieved?

■ Has the project been successfully signed off?

■ Do the processes work?

6.3 Staying there

The momentum generated during the project needs to be maintained within normal processes to ensure that they don't stagnate or even regress. It is also essential that the SAM processes are institutionalised and incorporated to become part of 'everyone's everyday job'. Another key element of process success is to establish within each of the SAM processes a culture of continuous improvement, so that the processes continue to develop and mature even after the implementation project is complete. The following activities will achieve this:

- Incorporate the new SAM changes and processes into job descriptions and roles throughout ICT and the business, making them part of 'everyone's everyday job'.

- Maintain the profile and momentum by establishing a process of continuous improvement in each of the SAM processes (the Deming cycle of 'Plan–Do–Check–Act').

- Prevent complacency and regression within the process by continually reinforcing the SAM key messages and by incorporating SAM issues and polices into information provided to all new starters.

- Continue with the monitoring, measurement and review of all measurements, metrics, KPIs and CSFs to ensure continued development of the maturity of processes.

- Continuously emphasise the importance of the SAM processes to all ICT and business personnel.

How do you know when you are staying there? Consider the following questions.

- Are SAM policies in place and are they adhered to?

- Is an appreciation of SAM part of the overall organisational culture?

- Is SAM information included in 'starter packs' and induction programmes for new starters?

- Is the number of exceptions detected reducing?

- Is the number of detected inaccuracies within the SAM database reducing?

- Is a process of continuous improvement operational in all areas of SAM?

6.4 Proving you are staying there

It is important that as well as preserving, if not improving, the quality of the SAM processes, time is spent proving that the processes are maintaining the necessary levels of quality, effectiveness, efficiency and protection required by the business and the organisation. The only method of proving that standards and quality are being maintained is by continuously carrying out the following processes:

- Conducting regular internal reviews and audits, and comparing the results against previous review exercises (minimum once per year, depending on the effectiveness of procedures for accurate record-keeping and Licence Management).

- Conducting regular external reviews and audits, and comparing the results against previous exercises and industry standards and benchmarks.

- Gaining and retaining accreditation and certification against industry 'best practice' and quality standards.

- Occasionally completing surprise or ad hoc reviews and audits.

- Developing and measuring metrics that demonstrate continuous improvement and trend year-on-year.

■ Implementing processes and procedures to deal with and rectify all inefficiencies and non-compliances identified during reviews and audits.

How do you know when you can prove you can stay there? Consider the following questions.

■ Have you got all of the information and records relating to all software assets?

■ If a software questioned your licence compliance are you confident you can provide information to satisfy them?

■ If you had an external audit are you confident you can provide all of the necessary licence information to satisfy the auditors?

■ Have you had supplier checks and were they satisfactory or were there any non-conformances?

■ Have you had external audits that gave positive feedback about your processes?

■ Have all issues of non-conformance from an audit been rectified?

■ Do your records match those of your suppliers/manufacturers?

7 TOOLS AND TECHNOLOGY

The appropriate use of tools within SAM processes is fundamental to their success. This chapter considers the types of tools that are available to assist with the effective management of software assets and how they can be used. The tools selected for each organisation will depend on many factors including in particular the platforms and technology already in place and the overall management-tool architecture.

SAM tool requirements should not be considered in isolation, but should be considered in conjunction with the overall requirement for management tools within the whole of ICT. This will ensure that whatever tools are purchased for use within SAM, processes can be integrated with other ICT Management tools as part of an overall management architecture. Tool selection and installation is covered in detail in Appendix C and in the ITIL *ICT Infrastructure Management* guide.

It is important before buying any tool that the right culture has been established within the organisation, and that people's roles and responsibilities have been determined. Often the implementation of a tool fails because the culture of the organisation is wrong or the processes are over-engineered, too bureaucratic or are not practical for certain user groups.

> **Key message**
>
> Tools should not be selected without having a clear understanding of how they will fit in with the culture of the organisation, and with the roles and responsibilities of the people involved. How they will be used also needs to be clear before selection, including the extent to which they fit existing processes, require changed processes, or require software customisation. For most environments, more than one tool will be required and in-depth knowledge of their deployment requirements will be necessary in their selection.

Figure 7.1 gives an overview of the SAM technology architecture, including the major types of tools available. Each of these is separately discussed in this chapter. There are many other tools available to support the ICT infrastructure, for example to cover other areas of ITIL such as Capacity Management and Release Management. A discussion of those tools is beyond the scope of this guide.

There is a technology dimension to the measures software manufacturers sometimes apply to try to ensure that their software is properly licensed and used in accordance with its terms and conditions. Understanding the relevant issues can help end users deal with these measures more effectively, and potentially gain additional value from them for internal purposes. These issues are discussed in Section 7.10.

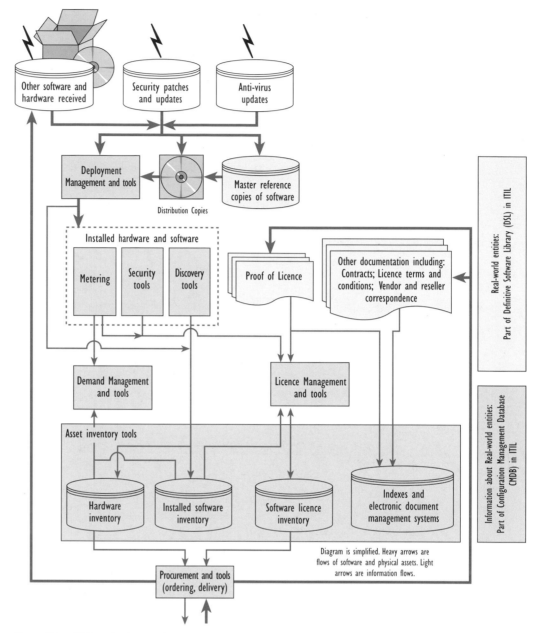

Figure 7.1 – SAM technology architecture

7.1 Asset inventory tools

Asset inventory tools are the essential foundation of all SAM activity. At the simpler end of the spectrum, a spreadsheet may constitute the asset inventory tool for a small organisation. However, a more extensive solution is normally to be expected.

Externally available software tools vary considerably in their functionality. At the top end, they are typically integrated with other functionality. Three broad categories of asset inventory functionality can be identified:

- **Inventories of hardware and installed software:** These are the most common types of tools, and are often integrated with, or designed to work with, discovery tools.

- **Inventories of software licences:** Available functionality for managing software licences is comparatively limited. Tools for inventories of hardware and installed software may include some licence inventory functionality. There are also more specialist Licence Management applications available. Basic functionality includes the linking of different types of licences purchased to the current licences available for use, and where the use of the licence is assigned. Other functionality can support procurement functions including the reallocation of licences between different operational units.

- **Document Management systems:** Other physical documentation such as contracts and correspondence also need to be managed and kept secure yet also made accessible. Electronic Document Management systems are best suited to doing this, and allow easy linking or cross-referencing to other database systems. Copies of physical proof of licence would typically also be held in the Document Management system, with the originals stored in a separate, secure location.

7.2 Discovery tools

Discovery tools are designed to find hardware and installed software and collect relevant details about them. Discovery tools are used during an initial implementation, and also periodically during ongoing operations as part of the 'Verification and audit' compliance process (see Paragraph 5.4.1).

There are a large number of tools in the market that address this area. Some of the major issues involved are:

- **Platform:** Discovery tools need to be able to audit software on a range of platforms. Often an organisation will have to use several different discovery tools because of the platform limitations of individual tools.

- **Networked vs. non-networked use:** Discovery tools are most efficient in a networked environment. However, there may be many machines that are seldom or never connected to a network, and methods must be found for getting information about these.

- **Method and reliability of software identification:** There are several methods of software identification, and tools may provide for a combination of them. In general all approaches work well for major commercial applications developed and installed in accordance with industry standards. They are less helpful for in-house applications and much popular software commonly distributed by the Internet, such as file swapping and instant messaging programs, which an organisation may wish to identify and remove.

  - Signatures: Some discovery tools utilise 'signature' information about the names, sizes, etc. of key files for particular applications. These tools depend on the signature files being updated to allow new software to be identified.
  - Internal file documentation: Well-designed commercial software following industry standards will now include internal fields that can be read by discovery software, without the need to have signature files. Programs that do not follow these standards will not be easily recognised.
  - Registry entries: Much software now also places entries in the system registry that

can be read by discovery tools. Major commercial packages and installation routines do this. However, other types of software may not comply.

- **Ability to summarise meaningfully:** An application may consist of hundreds or thousands of individual files, all covered by one licence. Alternatively, a single licence may be required for one file. Installations may be complete or partial. Updates and patches may be applied, potentially affecting large numbers of files. Installations may be uninstalled, but without removing all of the relevant files. Discovery tools differ greatly in how user-friendly and accurate they are in identifying specific applications and the state of installation of each application. Extensive manual effort may be required to turn the output of discovery tools into meaningful summary application information.

The output from discovery tools is often used as the basis for licence compliance assessment. However, such an approach may give the wrong results without a full understanding of how software is actually used and the relevant licensing terms and conditions. For example, an application may be installed on a server, where it would be discovered only once. However, it might be executed from the server by many people connected to it, each of whom might require a licence.

7.3 Metering tools

Metering tools are intended to measure active usage of a software product, rather than simply detect its existence as discovery tools do. When these tools are used just to monitor and report, they may be referred to as 'passive metering' tools. When they are used also to verify licences before running, they may be referred to as 'active metering' tools (especially for third-party products). (Terminology used by different tools may vary.)

Metering tools are historically most closely associated with monitoring the usage of server-based applications. Some licences are sold with 'concurrent usage' rights, which means that there is a maximum number of people who can use the software at any one time. Metering tools can be effective at providing absolute control against available licences in these cases. Alternatively, when the maximum is exceeded, an exception condition can be generated to initiate corrective action or the purchasing of additional licences.

Metering tools are increasingly being used to measure active usage on non-server devices, especially workstations. Some tools can even distinguish between active and minimised applications. With appropriate analysis, active usage information can help identify software that is installed but which is not being used actively. Decisions may be taken to redeploy licences being unnecessarily tied up in this way, rather than purchase yet more licences when they are needed elsewhere.

Licence verification functionality has also developed considerably. In particular, there are now a number of third-party tools providing these capabilities, referred to as active metering tools. These capabilities may be largely stand-alone, or incorporated in broader suites of products.

Metering tools require the same type of regular metric/signature updating as discovery tools. Metering will only produce meaningful information for those applications it has been set up to recognise.

A major consideration with metering tools is their performance overhead. Increasingly, there are also legal issues in countries where there are strong employee rights or workers' councils. In these countries, a metering tool may be considered a way of controlling the individual. The exact type of metering to be implemented may need to be assessed carefully, and done in consultation with the appropriate employee representative organisations.

7.4 Licence Management tools

Licence Management tools are potentially one of the most important tools in a SAM implementation, but the state of the market is comparatively immature. This function is largely manual in many organisations, and prone to error or not being done at all. Automation, to the extent that it exists, is often just for the different types of usage information, e.g. from discovery tools or from metering tools.

There are several types of functionality that may be considered necessary for a Licence Management tool:

- Being able to determine and track on a regular basis (without extensive manual work) the need for each type of licence based on the appropriate usage criteria. For example, the need for licences may be based on the number of installed copies; the total number of users; the maximum number of concurrent users; or the number of connected printers divided by five.
- Being able to demonstrate the effective licences held, which requires the linking of upgrade licences with the underlying full original licences.
- Being able to link licence requirements to effective licences held, and to report on licensing exceptions identified.
- Being able to manage 'stocks' of unused licences, and potentially negative 'stocks' if licences only need to be ordered periodically after the software is installed.
- Being able to facilitate the transfer of licences held to different operational units.

Ideally, Licence Management should be at the level of individual licences, linking specific licences to where those licences are used. Doing this may require linking different volume licences for different quantities of licences in complex ways.

7.5 Contract Management tools

Contract Management information is likely to be integrated with Licence Management information, since many detailed Licence Management issues link in to overall contractual issues. It may also be integrated with financial purchasing software. The types of functionality needed in this area include:

- warning about automatic contract extensions or maintenance payments due, deadlines for internally initiated renewals, etc.
- monitoring total purchasing levels against agreements to ensure that relevant commitments or projections are being met, for pricing purposes.

(Contract Management functionality is not shown in Figure 7.1.)

7.6 Demand Management tools

Demand Management can be viewed as an add-on capability for metering tools. The objective is to highlight software that is not being actively used over a given period, and for which it may be possible to save money by redeploying the underused licences.

7.7 Deployment Management tools

Deployment tool technology is comparatively well developed. The issue for SAM is to ensure that deployments are properly authorised, and that relevant deployment data is captured within the SAM database.

7.8 Security tools

There are a number of security issues that are particularly relevant to SAM, for which there are a number of tools available. There is considerable overlap between this area and that of security in general, and the two must be clearly coordinated for best results.

- **Installation security tools:** There are a number of approaches to controlling software installations, and preventing unauthorised installations. Some of these can be implemented at the operating system level. There are also some major packages that have extensive functionality for determining who can install and/or run which software. (There may be other related SAM functionality included, such as metering.)

- **Protection tools:** Anti-virus software can be viewed as a SAM concern, as can general protection measures meant to protect existing software assets from compromise. The main issue for the rest of SAM is to ensure that anti-virus and security patch update procedures are tightly integrated into the overall process for SAM, so that updates are distributed quickly and reliably when needed.

7.9 Procurement tools

Procurement is an important area for SAM. (See Paragraph 5.3.4.) Increasingly, procurement tools and solutions are being developed that are targeted at SAM benefits. Relevant capabilities include:

- ability to check on-line for the availability of unused licences as part of the ordering process, checking initially within the immediate operating entity, and then potentially with affiliated organisations that may have spare licences to transfer

- automatic linking of ordered licences to relevant licensee, e.g. PCs or individuals, to avoid repeat work later.

7.10 Vendor Licence Management technology

The focus of this guide is on customer management of software assets, including licensing. However, there are also a number of vendor (i.e. software manufacturer) technologies used directly by the manufacturer to help ensure proper licensing and use in accordance with terms and conditions. These may have infrastructure implications to ensure that the software continues to run.

- **Licensing keys:** Licensing keys are the most widely used approach to vendor-managed use, and generally the least effective at preventing unlicensed use. However, it may be possible to trace the source of keys on unauthorised copies, especially if the keys are unique to individual licences. Unauthorised use may come to the attention of software manufacturers in many ways, such as technical support calls by users with problems, during Internet connections to download updates, and as a result of audits.

- **Hardware dongles:** This is one of the simplest secure forms of Licence Management technology, with each program keyed to require a specific hardware dongle to be attached to the PC (or other equipment) for it to run.

- **Technical Licence Management:** With this technology, electronic licence certificates are obtained centrally and distributed to individual PCs/users/etc. as required. The product itself checks to see if the licence is available. Vendors may implement this type of technology to handle different architectures and build in flexibility for unlicensed use, e.g. granting a grace period before enforcement, or allowing a grace period if there is a licence certificate interruption. A licence server is normally required, either on-line for each execution or to provide a more permanent key that may be used when not connected.

- **Metering:** With this technology, the licensed product itself does no checking, but rather an independent monitoring agent identifies its (requested) execution and can record usage and also prevent execution. There are many ways of bypassing this type of control, but these may be partially addressed by protected logs which can be analysed, e.g. for completeness of time coverage.

- **Wrapper technology:** This technology encapsulates an application that cannot otherwise be controlled by technical Licence Management, so that the wrapper provides this functionality. The wrapper technology may impact on the maintainability of the product, e.g. the ability or the amount of time and work required to implement patches.

8 PARTNERS AND SAM

'Partner' is used here in the sense of organisations involved in a (potential) business relationship or association. This chapter highlights some of the ways that an organisation may use partners to support SAM implementations and ongoing SAM operations. Many of these possibilities are not generally recognised or understood. They may be significant factors in determining the ease with which SAM is implemented and operates.

In general, references are not made to any particular partners or sources. It is possible to find current information about many of these areas by using a good Internet search engine and entering key words or phrases like 'Software Asset Management', or by going to the websites of major partners of any of the types listed below.

The comments in this section are subjective, but are intended to give practical advice based on experienced views. There will be exceptions to the generalisations given here. Furthermore, the market will continue to develop, meaning that some of these comments will become obsolete over time.

The types of partners covered here are:

- software manufacturers/vendors
- resellers
- SAM tool vendors and implementers
- SAM consultants
- SAM outsourcers
- auditors
- IT research organisations
- professional and industry associations
- anti-piracy organisations.

Many partner organisations fulfil more than one of these roles. Suggested criteria for selecting partners are given in Appendix E, 'Choosing a SAM partner'.

The main types of deliverables available from partners are:

- SAM guidance materials, including 'best practice' guidelines
- SAM consultancy
- outsourcing of SAM functions
- audits
- certification
- conferences and workshops
- licensing advice
- historical purchase records and effective licensing
- current purchase records
- directories and assessments of SAM tools
- SAM tools
- implementation assistance for SAM tools.

Each of these is discussed in more detail below.

8.1 SAM guidance materials

There are a number of guides available about SAM, especially over the Internet from software manufacturers and anti-piracy organisations. Much of the focus is on licensing compliance issues for smaller organisations, rather than on the broader issues of comprehensive SAM.

Research organisations publish overview materials about various issues related to SAM, such as trends in the SAM tool marketplace, and total cost of ownership (TCO) issues.

8.2 SAM consultancy

At the time of writing this guide, SAM consultancy industry-wide is in its comparative infancy, but the area is developing quickly and is creating some of the 'best practice' described in this guide. Concerns about licence compliance drive much of this work. There is also a consultancy approach driven from the strategic procurement side, which tends to focus on quick wins in procurement arrangements and not on longer-term infrastructure projects. The most in-depth consultancy projects are generally associated with tool implementation.

SAM consultancy tends to be provided by highly experienced individuals, typically operating in small organisations or in small units of large organisations. Assessing the qualifications and suitability of a potential SAM consultant is not straightforward. See Appendix E for suggestions about how to approach this.

8.3 Outsourcing of SAM functions

Different types of outsourcing related to SAM are available, such as

- Application Service Provider (ASP)-type hosting and maintenance of specialist Licence Management applications.
- Capture of orders via an external provider order-entry application placed on the end-customer's intranet, linked to the reseller systems.
- Full ICT procurement processing via implants within an organisation, e.g. the ICT procurement function may be largely subcontracted to a specialist team from an outsourcer, but operating fully within the user organisation.
- Ongoing responsibility for full ICT asset discovery and inventory, to provide regularly updated information about ICT assets both to local management and to corporate management.

Outsourcing may be one of the fastest, most reliable, and most cost-effective ways of achieving SAM objectives. However, careful management is important as in all outsourcing situations. Some of the issues to consider are:

- Who has responsibility for ensuring licence compliance, and for handling the costs of possible licence compliance audits required by software manufacturers? (Legally, how effectively can the responsibility for licence compliance ever be passed to a third party, and what operational responsibilities therefore can be delegated appropriately?)

- Possible conflicts with other outsourcers and internal units in protection of perceived 'territories'.

- Possible conflicts of interest from the outsourcer, e.g. unwillingness to move to new technology or systems, or to improve problem areas, because of potential revenue impact or inflexible contracts. Also possible conflicts of interest if the outsourcer performs other functions, e.g. if it is a reseller.

- Establishing e-monitoring service levels.

8.4 Audits

Effective SAM cannot be achieved without auditing the machines hosting the software. Furthermore, a snapshot or one-off audit does not provide ongoing compliance. A continuous process is required to maintain control of the asset base.

The main types of audit related to SAM concern licence compliance. These may be conducted by:

- Software manufacturers directly.

- Independent third-party organisations on behalf of software organisations. Most often, independent accountancy firms are engaged by software manufacturers to conduct audits of licence compliance. (Many volume licensing agreements specifically provide for this.) These reviews may be invoked under the audit clauses of relevant licensing agreements, but more often they are mutually agreed with the end-user organisation and structured to provide coverage of broader SAM issues than just licence compliance. These reviews focus on the software of the software manufacturer.

- Independent third-party organisations on behalf of end-user organisations. A broad range of organisations (e.g. resellers, consultants, auditors) provide licensing audits directly for end-user organisations. These reviews tend to cover a broad range of software and hardware assets. They may be initiated based on pure internal requirements, as the result of a perceived risk of external review, or in connection with certification programs in some countries.

Section 8.5 deals with the subject of certification audits.

8.5 Certification

There are many types of certification available that relate to SAM, but their profile is relatively low. These are addressed in the following paragraphs.

8.5.1 SAM and licence compliance certifications

There are a small number of certification programmes around the world for licence compliance or SAM. These have generally been offered by or in association with software manufacturers or anti-piracy organisations. Such certifications at present have little legal weight. Their primary value is internal, to demonstrate a level of accomplishment in achieving SAM goals.

SAM and licence compliance certification programmes are appealing in principle, but have many difficulties associated with them:

- There have been no generally agreed standards for assessment of good SAM performance, and the difficulty of covering all of the relevant licensing programmes is great.

- Certification has particular value to an organisation if it means no manufacturer licensing audits for a period of time. However, this can also be viewed as giving *carte blanche* for new licensing breaches for that entire period, so manufacturers are wary of it. The wording on the certificates is therefore typically carefully limited.

- Certification is only as good as the skills of the certifiers, and for the areas covered.

Case study

A subsidiary of a multinational organisation obtained certification of its SAM systems from an anti-piracy organisation. The subsidiary was then audited by a software manufacturer and found to be substantially underlicensed. It had good administrative systems, but did not properly understand the terms of its organisation's global licensing agreements, and had not purchased necessary licences.

8.5.2   Personal certifications

The anti-piracy side of one industry software organisation has offered a personal qualification in Software Asset Management based on a short course and exam. Personal certifications are also available in a number of ICT areas that impact on SAM, from various sources.

Personal certifications may also be available from software manufacturers for their own licensing programmes. These are generally intended for reseller personnel, but it is worth an end-user organisation asking if these are available for its personnel as well.

8.5.3   General procedural certifications

There are various national and international standards such as ISO and 9001 that may be relevant to SAM. Each standards body has its own arrangements for awarding the certifications. The main limitations of such certifications for SAM purposes at present are:

- The scope of procedures covered does not have to include much, if anything, related to SAM.

- To the extent that SAM-related processes may be covered, there is little basis for the assessment of the adequacy of the procedures documented, but rather only compliance to them. As a result, certification may indicate compliance with poorly designed procedures.

8.6 Conferences and workshops

Professional and industry associations and research organisations are good sources of conferences and workshops addressing SAM or related issues. Almost all of the other types of partners also tend to stage conferences and workshops. These may be good venues for getting ideas and talking to people who have gone through the process of implementing SAM.

8.7 Licensing advice

Good licensing advice is a major factor in achieving licensing savings. Ultimately, the end-user organisation has the responsibility for its own licensing, so cannot place excessive reliance on external advice. Nonetheless, having good external sources of licensing advice is an important aide in recognising opportunities and minimising exposure.

Software manufacturers may offer detailed written guidance on their own licensing issues and these are often on their websites.

Overall, resellers are probably the best source of consistently accessible detailed licensing advice, although the variability in quality is great. When assessing a reseller (or other organisation) for its licensing advice, the rate of turnover of licensing specialist personnel should be considered. It is also a good idea to ask some detailed questions to see how well they can advise on specific licensing issues, and compare answers between different resellers. A good reseller will identify areas where money can be saved.

> **Example**
>
> One reseller advised a customer that the order they were placing for a major infrastructure upgrade was not required, because previously purchased upgrade insurance (forgotten by the customer) already provided the necessary upgrade rights.

Good resellers know the detailed considerations of software licensing conditions because they are experienced and specialise in these aspects, dealing with them on a daily basis.

8.8 Historical purchase records and effective licensing

For any organisation undertaking a SAM implementation, a major challenge is to determine what licences are already owned, because of historical problems of poor retention of proof of licence, and poor filing of old invoices.

Software manufacturers may be able to provide detailed information about historical purchases through volume licensing programs, for which the manufacturer normally records the name of the purchaser. The success of this approach will depend on the size of the requesting organisation, the specific manufacturer involved, sometimes on the geographical location of the manufacturer's office, and on the ease of identifying the records for the organisation that may have had name and organisational changes. (The names recorded on licensing records may be highly arbitrary depending on what the purchaser wrote down.) Nonetheless, this is one of the best potential sources of historical licensing information for most large organisations undertaking a SAM implementation. Having a copy of software manufacturer historical purchasing records will go some way towards addressing the problem of a lack of proof of licence for historical purchases. These purchase records do not constitute proof of licence, but it is unlikely that a software manufacturer would take legal action about licences it knew had been purchased.

There may be problems in making use of such data if there have been large-scale mergers or demergers. In such cases, a major exercise may be required to analyse the deployment and movement of licences over time, and to produce formal licence transfer documentation to regularise the situation. The value of licences found through such an exercise is typically much higher than an organisation will know by itself at the beginning of a SAM implementation.

Software manufacturers might also be able to provide an 'effective licensing' analysis of purchase records. This is an analysis of the different types of licences purchased, including upgrades and upgrade insurance, to determine the current effective licences which are owned, after all upgrades are applied to the respective underlying products.

Resellers may also be able to provide detailed information about historical purchases. The typical advantages of getting such information from resellers are:

- the data is often at a lower level of organisational detail than the manufacturer holds, allowing for better historical analysis and subsequent tracking
- the data covers all products sold by that reseller, not just a single software manufacturer.

The typical disadvantages are:

- often the data will not be available because the reseller has gone out of business, or systems have been converted leaving old data inaccessible
- the reseller may not be cooperative if they are no longer a major supplier to the organisation requesting the information
- the records have less credibility with the software manufacturer and potentially in court.

This third point is seldom stressed, but is important, because resellers may not always sell authentic products, or may not (accidentally or intentionally) report orders through to the manufacturer for volume licences. This is why a proof of licence produced by the manufacturer itself is always so important. In any case, it is worth asking the reseller for their data download. Any information obtained will almost always be useful, even if manufacturer data is also obtained, because of the additional reseller order detail compared to manufacturer information.

Some resellers, consultants and tool implementers might also be able to provide 'effective licensing' analyses of the licences purchased by an organisation, based on historical purchasing records. Typically, this would be a charged service.

The time and cost to retrieve and analyse historical purchase records could potentially be quite high. Therefore, an assessment should be made of the expected value of the licences that will be identified in this way, against the cost of performing the exercise.

8.9 Current purchase records

Regardless of the situation with historical purchase records, an organisation can benefit from arrangements to have access to current purchase records. These abilities depend significantly on the manufacturer and on the reseller, with a spectrum of different capabilities being available.

In some cases, on-line access is now available to manufacturer's systems to see current purchasing transactions. These systems may also provide proof of licence. This on-line customer access to manufacturers' records has proved very useful in Licence Management even in the absence of a more extensive SAM approach.

Resellers can also offer extensive capabilities in this area. Larger resellers, in particular, can offer larger organisations with multiple locations a way to allow decentralised ordering, but clear visibility from the centre of all purchasing activity, for all software manufacturers and also for hardware – as long as the decentralised locations use these facilities. These reporting facilities may also be associated with specialised order entry interfaces.

Some resellers can also offer a download capability into in-house SAM systems for recording all licences purchased, for use in Licence Management.

8.10 Directories and assessments of SAM tools

There is only a limited amount of information available about SAM tools. ICT research organisations provide some, including useful information about market trends and possible vendors' viability problems. There is also currently at least one major directory of SAM tools available from a software manufacturer's website. Additional information on the selection of SAM tools is contained in Appendix C.

There are also directories of tools available for other functionality of ITIL. For example, at the time of writing of this guide, there is such a directory on the website of the British Computer Society Configuration Management Specialist Group (www.bcs-cmsg.org.uk).

8.11 SAM tools

There are hundreds of tools with some sort of SAM capability, but in practice there is a more limited number of tools which are used widely for 'production' in larger organisations. Such tools may be identified by discussion with other organisations and with consultants, by web searches, and in directories as indicated above.

There is also a significant number of 'discovery' tools more readily available, sometimes for free download in their complete versions or for trial. The websites of manufacturers and of anti-piracy organisations are good places to check. Manufacturer discovery tools can be expected to cover at least that manufacturer's own software reasonably well.

Some SAM solutions exist that integrate the order process with an internal Licence Management system, to ensure that licences are not purchased unless needed. Some resellers can also offer specialised order placement interfaces. Typically this is by means of an Internet-based ordering application that ensures that the products being ordered are currently available from the manufacturer, and authorised for the customer (e.g. available under the customer's purchasing contract). See also Chapter 7.

8.12   Implementation assistance for SAM tools

Implementation assistance for SAM tools may be offered by tool manufacturers themselves, especially for the largest enterprise systems, or for much smaller manufacturers. However, assistance for many of the mid-range and longer-established SAM tools is often provided by consultancy organisations, including resellers.

8.13   Special considerations for reseller relationships

This section is written with the explicit knowledge of a large number of reseller and customer audits.

Software assets are complex assets to control for the organisation. They are not like pencils that can be bought in bulk and left on the shelf with little worry. Likewise, the reseller of software assets needs to have special skills, and, as an organisation starts to recognise the importance of software assets and of SAM, the importance of having a good reseller will be increasingly recognised.

Unfortunately, the focus of many procurement departments is primarily on price. Resellers competing for this trade cut margins paper-thin, and can become essentially nothing more than order-processing back offices. If the customer is fully on top of all licensing matters, that is fine. However, this is not the standard situation. The customer then has a significant risk of not recognising both major opportunities and major risks related to software assets. A factual observation is that there are many breakdowns in reseller processes in these situations, and many licensing problems encountered by customers. For example, a reseller may price software low, with the expectation of getting profit on related services. But the software sales unit will not be able to justify building good logistical systems or keeping skilled licensing personnel. The customer will be encouraged to do things that keep reseller processing costs low – like consolidating orders – which make SAM more difficult to achieve for the customer. The selection of a reseller should be based on more than price. A marginally higher cost should be more than offset by the benefits of better service and better licensing advice.

9 MAPPING SAM TO ITIL AND OTHER APPROACHES

There are many different approaches that can be used to manage, support and deliver ICT services to the organisation. Some are based on proprietary architectures and frameworks, others are based on open, non-proprietary standards and best practice guidelines. The three leading open guidelines and standards in this area are:

- the OGC's IT Infrastructure Library (ITIL)
- the British Standards Institution's (BSI) British Standard 15000 (BS 15000)
- the IT Governance Institute's Control Objectives for Information and related Technology (COBIT).

The following sections give a brief outline of SAM relationships to these open guidelines and standards, together with some of the major proprietary management standards. The key area within all of these standards is that of asset and Configuration Management. The scope of these processes differs within these standards. No single process has overall responsibility for all of the physical and logical aspects of asset and Configuration Management in these different standards/guidelines:

- In ITIL the responsibility principally lies within the Configuration Management, Release Management and Financial Management processes.
- In BS 15000, the responsibility also principally lies within the Configuration Management, Release Management and Financial Management processes.
- In COBIT the responsibility principally lies within the processes of 'Manage the IT Investment' and 'Manage the Configuration'.

In organisations where these processes are less well developed and integrated, it is possible that there is duplication of effort between the various processes or more likely, and more dangerously, gaps between the individual processes. In order for these processes to be successful within the organisation, these aspects of SAM should form part of the overall strategies and plans of the ICT unit.

> **Key message**
>
> It is imperative that there is end-to-end continuity and integration between the various constituent SAM processes, whether an organisation is based upon ITIL, BS 15000 or COBIT principles and guidelines.

The discussion of these issues and the mapping of SAM processes to these different approaches are considered in detail within the following sections.

9.1 SAM and ITIL

One of the most comprehensive guidelines on ICT Management is contained within the IT Infrastructure Library (ITIL). This is a library containing a distillation of 'best practice' guidelines on the processes involved in the management, support and delivery of quality ICT services.

A high-level mapping of SAM to ITIL is given in Section 1.11. This section gives additional detail about such mapping by reference to more detailed ITIL process diagrams.

The management of asset and configuration information is seen principally as part of the role of the Service Management disciplines of Service Support and Service Delivery. The role of the Service Support processes is far more significant with respect to the SAM processes than Service Delivery. An overview of these support processes is given in Figure 9.1.

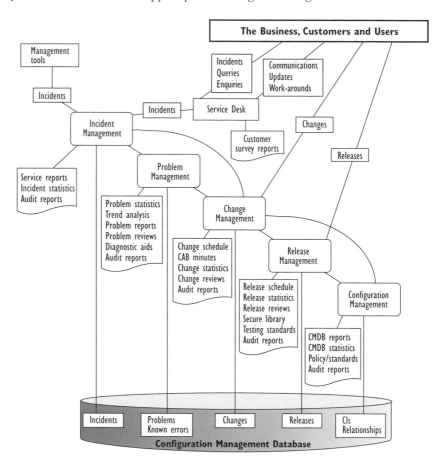

Figure 9.1 – The Service Support processes of ITIL

Configuration Management is a primary Service Support process and is of major significance to SAM. Configuration Management manages not only the assets and their associated lifecycles, but also the links and relationships between the assets. It also includes the management of relationships between these assets and other Service Management related issues such as incidents, problems and changes, Services and SLAs.

Management of the physical software assets of an organisation is considered to be one of the key roles of the Release Management process within ITIL. Thus, the control of the media, licence and authenticity documentation is all part of the remit of this process. (All of the financial aspects of Asset Management are within the scope of Financial Management, discussed separately below).

Asset Management within SAM is all of these aspects together. Asset Management, however, forms the basis of any good SAM system, and is best accomplished using a supporting relational database. The overall Asset Management processes within SAM include:

■ management of all aspects of software assets

- management of the associated hardware assets, to the extent necessary for SAM
- control and management of software components through all of the stages of their lifecycle
- management of software authenticity documentation and licences
- management of procurement and software contractual documentation
- storage and management of all master software media
- control and management of all installed copies of software
- management of the relationships between all of the above aspects
- the periodic reconciliation of the contents of the Definitive Software Library (DSL) with the contents of the Configuration Management Database (CMDB) with what is in use in the 'real world' live environment.

Between them, the ITIL Configuration Management and Release Management processes are responsible for all of the above SAM activities. ITIL recommends the use of a DSL and a CMDB for the management of software assets. Aspects of their involvement within the Asset Management process are illustrated in Figure 9.2.

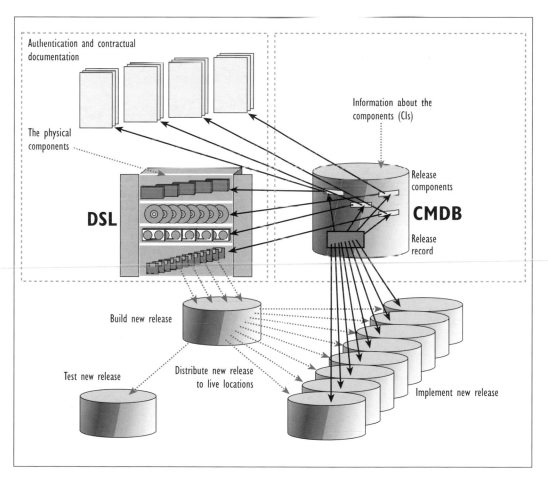

Figure 9.2 – ITIL use of the DSL and CMDB

In Figure 9.2, the dashed lines indicate the movement and deployment of physical components whereas the solid lines indicate the logical links and relationships contained within the CMDB. The design, development and implementation of these aspects of the process are crucial to the operation of efficient processes for the management of software assets. Within ITIL, each component contained within the CMDB is referred to as a Configuration Item (CI). Each CI record within the CMDB contains all of the attributes and information relating to a component necessary for managing it, whether software, hardware, contracts, etc.

The DSL acts as a single logical storage repository for all master copies of software in live use, or planned to be in live use within the organisation. Only quality-controlled software that has successfully completed all appropriate quality assurance checks should be registered and stored within the DSL. All authenticity and licence documentation should also be stored within the DSL. Scanned copies of these may also be stored within the CMDB. Within ITIL, the responsibility for the DSL resides within the Release Management process. This is also a fundamental requirement of good SAM processes. Generally, source code versions of in-house software are stored within the DSL, whereas for bought-in software executable versions are stored.

Other areas of ITIL Service Support that also involve elements of the SAM processes are:

- **Service Desk and** Incident Management: These are responsible within an ITIL-compliant organisation for the provision of a single point of contact for all users of ICT services and systems. Between them, they manage all incidents, issues, queries, requests and enquiries and must ensure that all anomalies relating to software assets, licences and their usage are reported immediately to the SAM processes for resolution and rectification or escalation.

- Problem Management: This is responsible within an ITIL-compliant organisation for the analysis of the root cause of incidents and problems and their subsequent prevention. SAM should work with Problem Management to ensure that all SAM exceptions are analysed to proactively prevent their recurrence.

- Change Management: This is responsible within an ITIL-compliant organisation for the management and control of all changes within an ICT environment. All changes involving software should be analysed for their impact on the SAM processes. They should then be managed through the stages of their lifecycle to ensure that all requirements of the SAM processes are satisfied, especially with regard to licence compliance and updating of the CMDB. The operation of an effective Change Management process is crucial to successful SAM processes.

The Service Delivery processes of Service Management also have a part to play in the SAM processes. These are illustrated in Figure 9.3. The role of these processes is not as significant as that of the support processes, but nonetheless they are significant in what they contribute.

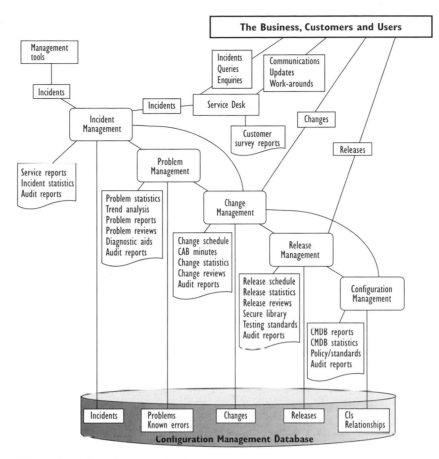

Figure 9.3 The Service Delivery processes of ITIL

The most significant of these delivery processes within the SAM area is that of Financial Management. The ITIL Financial Management processes are responsible for the management and control of all ICT related finances and costs. Details of all software procurement and actual expenditure should be collected and analysed by Financial Management, including all support and maintenance contracts, for incorporation into financial cost models. Financial Management should also be involved in the selection and negotiation of licence agreements, support contracts and the suppliers themselves to ensure that the most appropriate agreements are signed so that significant financial savings may be secured wherever possible.

The other Service Delivery processes that can contribute to the SAM processes are as follows:

- **Service Level Management (SLM):** This must ensure that all customer and user roles and responsibilities are agreed and documented within SLAs. Conditions must be included within all SLAs detailing that all users of ICT systems must accept, agree, sign and abide by the organisation's policies on software, security, and Internet usage, before using ICT systems and accessing ICT services.

- **Availability Management:** This might be involved where any software assets are responsible for causing service or component availability or unavailability issues.

- **IT Service Continuity Management (IT SCM):** This would need to ensure that all recovery and continuity plans are in place for all software in use within the organisation. Therefore, SAM processes should inform IT SCM of all new or changed software. Also IT SCM should ensure that all SAM issues have been addressed on all standby and recovery sites and systems.

■ **Security Management:** This would assist with the assessment of risk and the implementation of mitigation actions and countermeasures. Security Management should also assist with the detection, alerting and escalation of all software exceptions and non-compliance.

9.2 SAM and BS 15000

The BS 15000 standard is closely aligned with ITIL. Therefore the interfaces and dependencies that SAM has with the various processes involved are similar to many of those within ITIL. They are split into five separate areas:

■ **Service Delivery processes:** These are very similar in content to the Service Delivery processes of ITIL, but also additionally include Information Security Management and Service Reporting processes. They principally concern the development and improvement of the quality of ICT service delivered to the business.

■ **Control processes:** These consist of Configuration Management and Change Management.

■ **Release processes:** The Release Management process is the only process within this area.

■ **Resolution processes:** These consist of Incident and Problem Management processes.

■ **Relationship processes:** These consist of the Relationship Management processes relating to Supplier and Business Relationship Management.

The Control, Release and Resolution processes are similar to the ITIL Service Support processes involved in the day-to-day support and maintenance of ICT services and systems.

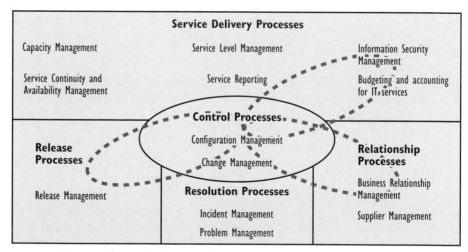

- - - - ■ The scope of Software Asset Management (SAM)
Figure reproduced from BS 15000–1/BS 15000–2 with the permission of the British Standards Institution

Figure 9.4 – Relationship between SAM and the BS 15000 Service Management processes

The principle areas of BS 15000 that interface with SAM are the Service Delivery, Control, Release and Relationship processes as illustrated in Figure 9.4, with the major areas being covered by the Configuration, Change and Release Management processes. Within BS 15000, responsibility for the CMDB, the DSL and the physical management of the media, licensing and authenticity documentation is all within the Configuration and Release Management processes.

Release Management is also responsible for the physical control and distribution of all software and hardware assets throughout the organisation, which is also a fundamental component of the SAM processes. It is essential that Release Management only distribute authentic software throughout the organisation for operational use and that all the relevant licences exist for all operational copies.

The Budgeting and Accounting process within the Service Delivery area also performs key financial elements of the SAM process functionality. The roles of the other processes within the Service Delivery processes, the Resolution processes and Control processes of BS 15000 are similar to their ITIL equivalents.

BS 15000 also includes the area of Relationship processes, consisting of the Business Relationship and Supplier Management processes. These also perform significant elements of the SAM process requirements.

- **Business Relationship Management (BRM):** This endeavours to establish and maintain good relationships with the business. It should involve educating the customers and ensuring that they understand their role within the SAM processes. Everyone within the organisation is responsible for complying with all of the policies relating to the use of ICT systems and services. It is BRM's role to develop a culture where this is understood and these policies are adhered to throughout the business.

- **Supplier Management:** This is the management of all suppliers including software suppliers, partners and resellers. In terms of SAM requirements, this process must guarantee that only reputable and responsible software suppliers are used to ensure that only authentic software is procured and that subsequently licences are secured from the actual software manufacturers. All interfaces and procedures with the suppliers should also be documented and adhered to.

9.3 SAM and COBIT

COBIT (Control Objectives for Information and related Technology. Copyright 1996, 1998, 2000, The IT Governance Institute[TM]) provides guidance on good practices for the management of IT processes in a manageable and logical structure. It has been produced by auditors as a set of processes and measures for the governance of ICT systems.

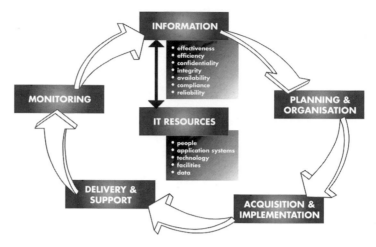

Figure 9.5 – The COBIT framework

The 34 processes of Care grouped into four separate domains as illustrated in Figure 9.5.
These areas and processes are as follows:

- **Planning and organisation:**
  - define a strategic IT plan
  - define the information architecture
  - determine the technological direction
  - define the IT organisation and relationships
  - manage the IT investment
  - communicate management aims and direction
  - manage human resources
  - ensure compliance with external requirements
  - assess risks
  - manage projects
  - manage quality.

- **Acquisition and implementation:**
  - identify automated solutions
  - acquire and maintain applications software
  - acquire and maintain technology infrastructure
  - develop and maintain procedures
  - install and accredit systems
  - manage changes.

- **Delivery and support:**
  - define and mange service levels
  - manage third-party services
  - manage performance and capacity
  - ensure continuous service
  - ensure system security
  - identify and allocate costs
  - educate and train users
  - assist and advise customers

- manage the configuration
- manage problems and incidents
- manage data
- manage facilities
- manage operations.

■ **Monitoring:**

- monitor the processes
- assess internal control adequacy
- obtain independent assurance
- provide for independent audit.

Because the functionality of ICT Management has been separated out into so many different processes, elements of SAM are covered in many more areas than is the case with either ITIL or BS 15000. These processes occur within all four domains of COBIT. However, the most significant SAM process within COBIT is that of 'Manage the Configuration'. The goal of this process is set out in the box.

> 'Accounting for all IT components, preventing unauthorised alteration, verifying physical existence and providing a basis for sound Change Management'

This process of 'Manage the Configuration' is a component of the 'Delivery and Support' domain within COBIT. It is one of the essential elements of COBIT and provides the basis for the operation of many of the other processes. It is very closely aligned with the Configuration Management processes of both ITIL and BS 15000. This process within COBIT provides:

- ■ an inventory of both hardware and software and the maintenance of all configuration information
- ■ the establishment of appropriate software libraries
- ■ enforcement of software authorisation and policies and Release Management policies
- ■ automated distribution, detection and checking mechanisms
- ■ integration with procurement, change and release processes
- ■ maintenance of configuration baselines, consistency and integration requirements

Clearly many of the above-listed activities are consistent with SAM processes and requirements. The other major area of COBIT responsible for significant aspects of SAM processes is 'Manage the IT Investment'. The key goals of this process are ensuring funding and controlling the disbursement of financial resources. The process is responsible for investment decisions, approving all expenditure and the recording and calculation of all costs associated with ICT systems and services.

Another process within the 'Manage the IT Investment' domain is that of 'Ensure compliance with external requirements'. The aim of this process is meeting legal, regulatory and contractual obligations and must ensure that all the necessary polices and procedures to achieve this have been documented, communicated and are regularly audited internally for compliance.

As can be seen from the lists of COBIT processes, there are many other areas that cover aspects of SAM processes, but the above two are the key areas of COBIT with respect to SAM.

9.4   SAM and other management frameworks and guidelines

There are several other frameworks and guidelines that have been developed for the management of ICT services and systems. These have principally been developed by hardware or software manufacturer and supplier organisations. Examples of these are:

- **HP,** with their IT Service Management (ITSM) reference model
- **IBM,** with their IT Process Model (ITPM) framework
- **Microsoft,** with their Microsoft Operations Framework (MOF) guidelines.
- **Sun,** with their Suntone framework.

These frameworks and guidelines have principally been based on or aligned with the ITIL framework and therefore the interactions between SAM and these frameworks have not been considered in any further detail within this guide.

10 BIBLIOGRAPHY

Note: the entries in this bibliography are given in alphabetical order of title within each section.

10.1 Associated reference books and documents

Application Management
OGC 2002
Available from TSO, www.tso.co.uk
ISBN 0-11-330866-3

The Business Perspective
OGC (To be published 2003)
Available from TSO, www.tso.co.uk
ISBN 0-11-330894-9

ICT Infrastructure Management
OGC 2002
Available from TSO, www.tso.co.uk
ISBN 0 11-330865-5

Managing Successful Projects with PRINCE2
OGC 2002
Available from TSO, www.tso.co.uk
ISBN 0-11-330891-4

Planning to Implement Service Management
OGC 2002
Available from TSO, www.tso.co.uk
ISBN 0-11-330877-9

Security Management
OGC 1999
Available from TSO, www.tso.co.uk
ISBN 0-11-330014-X

Service Delivery
OGC 2001
Available from TSO, www.tso.co.uk
ISBN 0-11-330015-8

Service Support
OGC 2001
Available from TSO, www.tso.co.uk
ISBN 0-11-330017-4

10.2 Appropriate guidelines and standards

BS 15000–1:2002, IT Service Management (Part 1: Specification for Service Management)

BS 15000–2:2003, IT Service Management (Part 2: Code of practice for IT Service Management)

PD 0005:2003, IT Service Management: A Manager's Guide

PD 0015:2002, IT Service Management – Self assessment workbook

Website at www.bsi.org.uk

COBIT Executive Summary (3rd Edition, July 2000)
ISBN 1-893209-15-6

COBIT Framework (3rd Edition, July 2000)
ISBN 1-893209-14-8

COBIT Management Guidelines (3rd Edition, July 2000)
ISBN 1-893209-12-1

COBIT Control Objectives (3rd Edition, July 2000)
ISBN 1-893209-17-2
Website at http://www.isaca.org/cobit.htm

APPENDIX A TERMINOLOGY

A.1 Acronyms used in this guide

ASP	Application Service Provider
BS	British Standard
BRM	Business Relationship Management
BSA	Business Software Alliance
CAL	Client Access Licence
CBA	Cost Benefit Analysis
CMU	Customer Managed Use
COA	Certificate of Authenticity
CobiT®	Control Objectives for Information and related Technology. Copyright 1996, 1998, 2000, The IT Governance Institute™
CI	Configuration Item
CMDB	Configuration Management Database
CRM	Customer Relationship Management
CSF	Critical Success Factor
DSL	Definitive Software Library
EULA	End-User Licence Agreement
FAST	Federation Against Software Theft
ICT	Information and Communications Technologies
IoD	Institute of Directors
ISO	International Standards Organisation
ITIL	Information Technology Infrastructure Library
IT SCM	IT Service Continuity Management
IT SMF	IT Service Management Forum
KPI	Key Performance Indicator
OEM	Original Equipment Manufacturer
OGC	Office of Government Commerce
OLA	Operational Level Agreement
PDA	Personal Digital Assistant

ROI	Return on Investment
SAM	Software Asset Management
SIIA	Software & Information Industry Association
SLA	Service Level Agreement
SLM	Service Level Management
SLR	Service Level Requirement
SoR	Statement of Requirements
SPA	Software Publishers Association
TCO	Total cost of ownership
ToR	Terms of Reference
VAR	Value Added Reseller
VMU	Vendor Managed Use

A.2   Glossary of terms

Alert

Warning that an incident has occurred.

Asset

Component of a business process. Assets can include people, accommodation, computer systems, software, networks, paper records, fax machines, etc.

Asset Management

All of the processes involved in managing an organisation's ICT assets.

Availability

Ability of a component or service to perform its required function at a stated instant or over a stated period of time. It is usually expressed as the availability percentage, i.e. the percentage of time that the service is actually available for use by the customers within the agreed service hours.

Availability Management

The process of defining, determining, measuring and improving all aspects of the availability of IT services.

Balanced scorecard

An aid to organisational Performance Management. It helps to focus, not only on the financial targets but also on the internal processes, customers and learning and growth issues.

Baseline

A snapshot or a position that is recorded. Although the position may be updated later, the baseline remains unchanged and available as a reference of the original state and as a comparison against the current position (PRINCE 2).

Baseline security

> The security level adopted by the ICT organisation for its own security and from the point of view of good 'due diligence'.

BS 15000

> The British Standard for Service Management. This standard provides a comprehensive set of controls comprising best practices in the delivery of managed IT services.

BS 7799

> The British Standard for Information Security Management. This standard provides a comprehensive set of controls comprising best practices in information security.

Budgeting

> Budgeting is the process of predicting and controlling the spending of money within the organisation and consists of a periodic negotiation cycle to set budgets (usually annual) and the day-to-day monitoring of current budgets.

Build

> The final stage in producing a usable configuration. The process involves taking one or more input Configuration Items and processing them (building them) to create one or more output Configuration Items, e.g. software compile and load.

Business case

> A document examining all of the benefits, options, issues, risks, cost and problems associated with the implementation of a business solution.

Business function

> A business unit within an organisation, e.g. a department, division, branch.

Business process

> A group of business activities undertaken by an organisation in pursuit of a common goal. Typical business processes include receiving orders, marketing services, selling products, delivering services, distributing products, invoicing for services, accounting for money received. A business process usually depends upon several business functions for support, e.g. IT, personnel, accommodation. A business process rarely operates in isolation, i.e. other business processes will depend on it and it will depend on other processes.

Business recovery plans

> Documents describing the roles, responsibilities and actions necessary to resume business processes following a business disruption.

Business unit

> A segment of the business entity by which revenues are received and expenditure is caused or controlled, such revenues and expenditure being used to evaluate segmental performance.

Category

> Classification of a group of Configuration Items, change documents or problems.

Capacity Management

> The Service Management process tasked with defining the business' requirements for IT capacity, in both business and technical terms, and understanding and presenting the

consequences of delivering those volumes of activities through the IT Infrastructure at the right time and at optimal cost.

Change

The addition, modification or removal of approved, supported or baselined hardware, network, software, application, environment, system, desktop build or associated documentation.

Change Advisory Board (CAB)

A group of people who can give expert advice to Change Management on the implementation of changes. This board is likely to be made up of representatives from all areas within ICT and representatives from business units.

Change Authority

A group that is given the authority to approve change, e.g. by the project board. Sometimes referred to as the Configuration Board

Change control

The procedure to ensure that all changes are controlled, including the submission, analysis, decision-making, approval, implementation and post implementation of the change.

Change history

Auditable information that records, for example, what was done, when, who did it and why.

Change log

A log of Requests for change raised during the project, showing information on each change, its evaluation, what decisions have been made and its current status, e.g. Raised, Reviewed, Approved, Implemented, Closed.

Change Management

Process of controlling changes to the infrastructure or any aspect of services, in a controlled manner, enabling approved changes with minimum disruption.

Change record

A record containing details of which Configuration Items are affected by an authorised change (planned or implemented) and how.

Charging

The process of establishing charges in respect of business units, and raising the relevant invoices for recovery from customers.

Classification

A process of formally grouping Configuration Items or changes by type, e.g. software, hardware, or of formally identifying incidents, problems and known errors by origin, symptoms or cause.

Client Access Licence (CAL)

A licence that permits a client (e.g. a workstation) to access software services on a server. Often there will not be any special software on the client PCs, so the use of this type of licence cannot be measured by counting the installed copies of software. The number of licences required may be determined in different ways depending on the software manufacturer's terms and conditions. For example, it may be necessary to count client PCs, or to count the number of total users.

Compliance

The process of monitoring and enforcing a policy and a set of processes ensuring that there is no non-conformance.

Configuration baseline (see also Baseline)

Configuration of a product or system established at a specific point in time, which captures both the structure and details of the product or system, and enables that product or system to be rebuilt at a later date.

Configuration control

Activities comprising the control of changes to Configuration Items after formally establishing the configuration documents. It includes the evaluation, coordination, approval or rejection of changes. The implementation of changes includes changes, deviations and waivers that impact on the configuration.

Configuration documentation

Documents that define requirements, system design, build, production, and verification for a configuration item.

Configuration identification

Activities that determine the product structure, the selection of Configuration Items, and the documentation of the Configuration Items' physical and functional characteristics including interfaces and subsequent changes. It includes the allocation of identification characters or numbers to the Configuration Items and their documents. It also includes the unique numbering of configuration control forms associated with changes and problems.

Configuration Item (CI)

Component of an infrastructure – or an item, such as a Request for Change, associated with an infrastructure – that is (or is to be) under the control of Configuration Management. CIs may vary widely in complexity, size and type, from an entire system (including all hardware, software and documentation) to a single module or a minor hardware component.

Configuration Management

The process of identifying and defining the Configuration Items in a system, recording and reporting the status of Configuration Items and Requests for Change, and verifying the completeness and correctness of configuration items.

Configuration Management Database (CMDB)

A database that contains all relevant details of each CI and details of the important relationships between CIs.

Configuration structure

A hierarchy of all the CIs that comprise a configuration.

Continuous Service Improvement Programme

An ongoing formal programme undertaken within an organisation to identify and introduce measurable improvements within a specified work area or work process.

Control Objectives for Information and related Technology (CobiT®)

Copyright 1996, 1998, 2000, The IT Governance Institute™. Provides guidance and good practices for the management of IT processes.

Cost

The amount of expenditure (actual or notional) incurred on, or attributable to, a specific activity or business unit.

Cost-Benefit Analysis (CBA)

An activity designed to analyse and compare the costs and the benefits involved in a certain course of action to determine its feasibility. (**see also Feasibility Study**).

Cost-effective

Ensuring that there is a proper balance between the quality of service on the one side and expenditure on the other. Any investment that increases the costs of providing ICT services should always result in enhancement to service quality or quantity.

Cost of failure

A technique used to evaluate and measure the cost of failed actions and activities. It can be measured as a total within a period or an average per failure. An example would be 'the cost of failed changes per month' or 'the average cost of a failed change'

Costing

The process of identifying the costs of the business and of breaking them down and relating them to the various activities of the organisation.

Countermeasure

A check or restraint on the service designed to enhance security by reducing the risk of an attack (by reducing either the threat or the vulnerability), reducing the impact of an attack, detecting the occurrence of an attack and/or assisting in the recovery from an attack.

Crisis Management

The processes by which an organisation manages the wider impact of a disaster, such as adverse media coverage.

Critical Success Factor (CSF)

A measure of success or maturity of a project or process. It can be a state, a deliverable or a milestone. An example of a CSF would be 'the production of an overall technology strategy'.

Customer

Recipient of the service, usually the customer management has responsibility for the cost of the service, either directly through charging or indirectly in terms of demonstrable business need.

Customer-Managed Use (CMU)

The concept of customers managing their own use of licences, as opposed to the concept of Vendor-Managed Use (VMU). The focus of this guide is CMU.

Definitive Software Library (DSL)

The library in which the definitive authorised versions of all software CIs are stored and protected. It is a physical library or storage repository where master copies of software versions are placed, as well as other 'physical' assets such as proof of licence. This one logical storage area may in reality consist of one or more physical software libraries or file stores.

Dependency

The reliance, either direct or indirect, of one process or activity upon another.

Depreciation

The loss in value of an asset due to its use and/or the passage of time. The annual depreciation charge in accounts represents the amount of capital assets used up in the accounting period. It is charged in the cost accounts to ensure that the cost of capital equipment is reflected in the unit costs of the services provided using the equipment. There are various methods of calculating depreciation for the period, but the Treasury usually recommends the use of current cost asset valuation as the basis for the depreciation charge.

Disaster recovery planning

A series of processes that focus only upon the recovery processes, principally in response to physical disasters, which are contained within BCM.

Downtime

Total period that a service or component is not operational, within agreed service times.

End user

See 'User'

Environment

A collection of hardware, software, network communications and procedures that work together to provide a discrete type of computer service. There may be one or more environments on a physical platform, e.g. test or production. An environment has unique features and characteristics that dictate how it is administered in similar yet diverse manners.

External target

One of the measures against which a delivered ICT service is compared, expressed in terms of the customer's business.

Feasibility study

An activity designed to assess the feasibility of a certain course of action to determine its value to the business. (**See also Cost-Benefit Analysis**)

Financial Management

All the procedures, tasks and deliverables that are needed to fulfil an organisation's budgeting, accounting and charging requirements.

Financial year

An accounting period covering 12 consecutive months. In the public sector, this financial year generally coincides with the fiscal year, which runs from 1 April to 31 March.

ICT infrastructure

The sum of an organisation's ICT-related hardware, software, data telecommunication facilities, procedures and documentation.

ICT service

A described set of facilities, ICT and non-ICT, supported by the IT service provider, that fulfils one or more needs of the customer and that is perceived by the customer as a coherent whole.

Impact

Measure of the business criticality of an incident. Often equal to the extent to which an incident leads to distortion of agreed or expected service levels.

Incident

Any event which is not part of the standard operation of a service and which causes, or may cause, an interruption to, or a reduction in, the quality of that service.

Incident Management

The process of managing all unexpected operational events with the primary objective of restoring service to customers as quickly as possible.

Information and Communications Technologies (ICT)

The convergence of Information Technology, Telecommunications and Data Networking Technologies into a single technology.

Internal target

One of the measures against which supporting processes for the ICT service is compared. Usually expressed in technical terms relating directly to the underpinning service being measured.

ISO9001

The internationally accepted set of standards concerning Quality Management systems.

IT accounting

The set of processes that enable the IT organisation to account fully for the way money is spent (particularly the ability to identify costs by customer, service and activity).

IT directorate

That part of an organisation charged with developing and delivering the ICT services.

IT Service Continuity Management

The process of assessing and managing risks to IT services by examining CI values, threats and vulnerabilities, developing appropriate countermeasures, creating an IT Services Continuity plan and managing any disasters that occur.

IT service provider

The role of IT service provider is performed by any organisational units, whether internal or external, that deliver and support IT services to a customer.

IT Infrastructure Library (ITIL)

The OGC IT Infrastructure Library is a set of guides providing proven best practices, derived from user and vendor experts in both the private and public sectors, worldwide. Accepted as the *de facto* standard for ITSM processes.

Key Performance Indicator (KPI)

A measurable quantity against which specific performance criteria can be set when drawing up the SLA.

Key Success Indicator

A measurement of success or maturity of a project or process. (**See CSF**)

Known error

> An incident or problem for which the root cause is known and for which a temporary work-around or a permanent alternative has been identified. If a business case exists, an RFC will be raised, but, in any event, it remains a known error unless it is permanently fixed by a change.

Lifecycle

> A series of states, connected by allowable transitions. The lifecycle represents an approval process for Configuration items, problem reports and change documents

Metric

> Measurable element of a service process or function.

Novation

> The formal process of substituting legal obligations, e.g. changing one party to a contract for another when the original party has gone out of legal existence to be replaced by a new one.

Operational costs

> Those costs resulting from the day-to-day running of the ICT Services section, e.g. staff costs, hardware maintenance and electricity, and relating to repeating payments whose effects can be measured within a short timeframe, usually less than the 12-month financial year.

Operational Level Agreement (OLA)

> An internal agreement covering the delivery of services which supports the ICT organisation in their delivery of services.

Operations

> All activities and measures to enable and/or maintain the intended use of the ICT infrastructure.

Organisational culture

> The whole of the ideas, corporate values, beliefs, practices, expectations about behaviour and daily customs that are shared by the employees in an organisation.

Outsourcing

> The process by which functions performed by the organisation are contracted out for operation, on the organisation's behalf, by third parties.

PD0005

> Alternative title for the BSI publication *IT Service Management: A Manager's Guide.*

Performance criteria

> The expected levels of achievement, which are set within the SLA against specific Key Performance Indicators.

PRINCE2

> The standard UK Government method for Project Management

Priority

> Sequence in which an incident or problem needs to be resolved, based on impact and urgency.

Problem

> Unknown underlying cause of one or more incidents.

Problem Management

> Process that minimises the effect on customers of defects in services and within the infrastructure, human errors and external events.

Process(es)

> A connected series of actions, activities, changes, etc. performed by agents with the intent of satisfying a purpose or achieving a goal.

Process control

> The process of planning and regulating, with the objective of performing the process in an effective and efficient way.

Programme

> A collection of activities and projects that collectively implement a new corporate requirement or function.

Provider

> The organisation concerned with the provision of ICT services.

Quality of service

> An agreed or contracted level of service between a service customer and a service provider.

Release

> A collection of new and/or changed CIs, which are tested and introduced into the live environment together.

Release Management

> The process of planning, designing, building, configuring and testing hardware and software releases and planning, scheduling and implementing the controlled roll-out of authorised releases.

Request for Change (RFC)

> Form, or screen, used to record details of a request for a change to any CI within an infrastructure or to procedures and items associated with the infrastructure.

Resolution

> Action that will resolve an incident. This may be a work-around.

Resources

> The ICT Services section needs to provide the customers with the required services. The resources are typically computer and related equipment, software, facilities or organisational (people).

Return on investment (ROI)

> The ratio of the cost of implementing a project, product or service and the savings as a result of completing the activity in terms of either internal savings, increased external revenue or a combination of the two. For instance, in simplistic terms, if the internal cost of ICT cabling of office moves is £100,000 per annum and a structured cabling system can be installed for £300,000, then an ROI will be achieved after approximately three years.

Risk

> A measure of the exposure to which an organisation may be subjected. This is a combination of the likelihood of a business disruption occurring and the possible loss that may result from such business disruption.

Risk analysis

> The identification and assessment of the level (measure) of the risks calculated from the assessed values of assets and the assessed levels of threats to, and vulnerabilities of, those assets.

Risk management

> The identification, selection and adoption of countermeasures justified by the identified risks to assets in terms of their potential impact upon services if failure occurs, and the reduction of those risks to an acceptable level.

Risk reduction measures

> Measures taken to reduce the likelihood or consequences of a business disruption occurring (as opposed to planning to recover after a disruption).

Role

> A set of responsibilities, activities and authorisations.

SAM

> Software Asset Management (SAM) is all of the infrastructure and processes necessary for the effective management, control and protection of the software assets within an organisation, throughout all stages of their lifecycle.

SAM database

> A database set containing all of the necessary information to support the effective operation of all SAM processes and the management of all software assets. It could form part of an overall CMDB

Security Management

> The process of managing a defined level of security of information and services.

Security Manager

> The Security Manager is responsible for the Security Management process in the service provider organisation. The person is responsible for fulfilling the security demands as specified in the SLA, either directly or through delegation by the Service Level Manager. The Security Officer and the Security Manager work closely together.

Security Officer

> The Security Officer is responsible for assessing the business risks and setting the security policy. As such, this role is the counterpart of the Security Manager and resides in the customer's business organisation. The Security Officer and the Security Manager work closely together.

Service

> One or more ICT systems that enable a business process.

Service achievement

> The actual service levels delivered by the ICT organisation to a customer within a defined lifespan.

Service catalogue

> Written statement of ICT services, default levels and options.

Service Desk

> The single point of contact within the ICT organisation for users of ICT services.

Service Improvement Programme (SIP)

> A formal project undertaken within an organisation to identify and introduce measurable improvements within a specified work area or work process.

Service level

> The expression of an aspect of a service in definitive and quantifiable terms.

Service Level Agreement (SLA)

> Written agreement between a service provider and the customer(s) that documents agreed service levels for a service.

Service Level Management (SLM)

> The process of defining, agreeing, documenting and managing the levels of customer ICT service that are required and cost-justified.

Service Level Requirement (SLR)

> An agreement jointly produced by a service provider and customer(s) that documents the proposed service levels and responsibilities for an intended new or changed service.

Service Management

> Management of Services to meet the customer's requirements.

Service provider

> Third-party organisation supplying services or products to customers.

Service quality plan

> The written plan and specification of internal targets designed to guarantee the agreed service levels.

Service request

> Every incident not being a failure in the ICT Infrastructure.

Services

> The deliverables of the ICT Services organisation as perceived by the customers. The services do not consist merely of making computer resources available for customers to use.

Software Asset Management (SAM)

> All of the infrastructure and process necessary for the effective management, control and protection of the software assets within an organisation, throughout all stages of their lifecycle.

Software Configuration Item (SCI)

> As 'Configuration Item', excluding hardware and services.

Software environment

> Software used to support the application such as operating system, database management system, development tools, compilers, and application software.

Software library

> A controlled collection of SCIs designated to keep those with like status and type together and segregated from unlike, to aid in development, operation and maintenance.

Software work unit

> Software work is a generic term devised to represent a common base on which all calculations for workload usage and ICT resource capacity are then based. A unit of software work for I/O type equipment equals the number of bytes transferred, and for central processors it is based on the product of power and CPU-time.

Stakeholder

> Any individual or group who has an interest, or 'stake', in the ICT service organisation.

Stand-by arrangements

> Arrangements to have available assets, which have been identified as replacements should primary assets be unavailable, following a business disruption. Typically, these include accommodation, ICT systems and networks, telecommunications and sometimes people.

Statement of requirements (SoR)

> A document detailing all of the requirements for a new or revised business process.

Storage occupancy

> A defined measurement unit that is used for storage type equipment to measure usage. The unit value equals the number of bytes stored.

System

> An integrated composite that consists of one or more of the processes, hardware, software, facilities and people, providing a capability to satisfy a stated need or objective.

Third-party supplier

> An enterprise or group, external to the customer's enterprise, which provides services and/or products to that customer's enterprise.

Threat

> An indication of an unwanted incident that could impinge on the system in some way. Threats may be deliberate (e.g. wilful damage) or accidental (e.g. operator error).

Total cost Of ownership (TCO)

> Calculated including depreciation, maintenance, staff costs, accommodation, and planned renewal.

Underpinning contract

> A contract with an external supplier covering delivery of services that support the ICT organisation.

Unit costs

> Costs distributed over individual component usage. For example, it can be assumed that, if a box of paper with 1000 sheets costs £10, then each sheet costs 1p. Similarly if a CPU costs £1 million a year and it is used to process 1,000 jobs that year, each job costs on average £1,000.

Urgency

> Measure of the business criticality of an incident or problem based on the impact and on the business needs of the customer.

User

> The person who uses the service on a day-to-day basis.

Vendor-Managed Use (VMU)

> The concept of vendors (i.e., software manufacturers) managing customers' use of licences, as opposed to the concept of Customer-Managed Use (CMU). See Section 7.10 for a discussion of some VMU technologies.

Version

> An identified instance of a Configuration Item within a product breakdown structure or configuration structure for the purpose of tracking and auditing change history. Also used for Software Configuration Items to define a specific identification released in development for drafting, review or modification, test or production.

Version identifier

> A version number, version date, or version date and time stamp.

Vulnerability

> A weakness of the system and its assets, which could be exploited by threats.

APPENDIX B SOFTWARE LICENSING OVERVIEW

Software licensing is complex. Compliance with all of its terms and conditions requires in-depth knowledge. Typically, an organisation will need to assign the responsibility for understanding licensing to specific individuals, and then ensure that they have the necessary training (initial and ongoing) to master the area.

This guide cannot act as a substitute to an organisation understanding its own licensing terms and conditions. However, this appendix is intended to give the flavour of the complexity that can be found in software licensing.

Note: All comments in this section are generic, and may not correspond to specific terms and conditions of particular software.

B.1 When licences are required

Software licences are rights to use software, with certain terms and conditions attached, and are one of the main issues addressed by Software Asset Management. These rights to use software are totally separate from the legal rights to the software itself, which are normally kept by the software manufacturer or other third party. Licences may be bought, or may be 'free' subject to special terms and conditions. Even 'open-source' software normally has a licence, even though payment may not be required.

Licences are normally required whenever externally sourced software is 'used', which will typically be defined as either being installed on a machine, or as being executed on a machine, even if installed elsewhere (e.g. a server). They may also be defined in 'enterprise' terms, such as number of workstations or employees, in which case a licence is required for each qualifying unit or individual regardless of actual 'usage'.

Even with commercial software, there are several situations where paid licences may not be required, depending on specific contractual conditions. Often, these situations are not understood and, as a result, organisations may purchase licences they do not need. These situations include: workstations used for dedicated training purposes (with limits on numbers), copies used for evaluation purposes (with conditions on how they are used, and for how long) and copies used for distribution purposes. Likewise, there can be 'runtime' versions of some software, which do not require separate paid licences. (It may be difficult to distinguish between runtime and non-runtime versions of such software.)

Backups are problematical legally. Many software contracts only allow for one backup copy for archival purposes, but this is contrary to good IT practice for making backups. However, it is unlikely that a software manufacturer would make an issue of this, or that a court would uphold it if taken that far. The critical issue is that the copies should be purely for backup purposes, with no more copies ever being used (installed or executed) than are licensed. The situation for 'hot' backups is different, because in these cases the backup software is installed. Reference must be made to specific licence terms and conditions in these cases.

B.2 Basic types of licences

Licences can have many different characteristics for description purposes:

B.2.1 Duration

- **Perpetual:** Historically, most licences sold have been perpetual, i.e. the use rights are permanent once purchased.

- **Subscription or rental:** Licences that can be used for a specific period of time, which can vary from days to years and may or may not include upgrade rights.

- **Temporary:** in addition to subscription or rental licences, there can be other cases of temporary licences, e.g. pending full payment or receipt of proof of licence.

B.2.2 Measure of usage

- **Per copy: by workstation/seat/device, named user, anonymous user, concurrent user:** Historically, most licences sold have been on a per-copy-used basis, with several different units of measure possible. Sometimes multiple uses will be allowed per licence (e.g. for some PC-linking software). It should also be noted that licensing is sometimes based on unit counts other than just PCs. For example, printer counts are important in several licensing schemes, e.g. for fonts (where there may be a limit on the number of printers that can download the fonts per licence), and for some networking software node counts. Likewise, mobile devices (PDAs, SmartPhones, etc.) have licensing requirements but may not be recognised by many 'traditional' approaches to Licence Management based just on PCs.

- **Concurrent usage:** This allows a specified number of users to connect simultaneously to a software application. This is a commonly understood licensing approach, and there are a number of software products to help monitor and control concurrent usage. However, such licences are not as commonly available as previously was the case.

- **Per server speed or per processor:** These are linked to the speed or power of the server on which they are run, or the number of processors within the server.

- **Client/server access:** Most licences correspond to physical installations or use of software. However, there is an important category of licences that do not correspond to physical software, and these are frequently misunderstood. These are client access licences, which give a client device the right to access a server package, regardless of whether or not there is client software associated with it. The detailed terms and conditions for such licences prevent software 'tricks' to combine multiple clients into a single channel for licensing purposes.

- **Enterprise or site:** Increasingly, licences are being sold on an enterprise or site basis that requires just a count of qualifying entities (workstations or employees, most commonly). This is usually easier for administration purposes, especially in organisations with limited SAM capabilities. Nonetheless, people who do not understand the contractual definition of the enterprise may try to apply 'per-copy' counting rules instead. A further complication may be that qualifying workstations or employees/contractors may not be simple to identify.

B.2.3   Upgrades

There are many different types of upgrades that have been sold, each typically with detailed conditions as to what is acceptable as a basis for the upgrade. A common problem is that upgrade licences are purchased, for which there are no qualifying underlying licences, e.g. competitive upgrades may have been purchased without any competitive product actually being owned, in which case the licences are invalid for use.

- Version upgrades normally refer to a later release of the same product.

- Product upgrades normally refer to changes within a product family, e.g. a partial suite of products being upgraded to a more extensive suite of the same product family.

- Competitive upgrades normally refer to upgrades based on competitive products.

- Language upgrades allow the use of a more expensive product with different/additional language capabilities.

- Upgrade insurance (maintenance, etc.). Many software manufacturers offer upgrade 'insurance' under a variety of names. Essentially, they all allow the purchasers to use any upgrades that are released during the period of the insurance. A problem that occurs sometimes is that organisations forget the upgrade rights they purchased with this insurance because they do not perform the physical upgrade during the same time period. They may then purchase the upgrades again later when the physical upgrade is performed.

- Technology guarantees, etc. Technology guarantees are limited-duration upgrade rights that a software manufacturer may grant to purchasers of one version of software, when a new version is expected but not yet released. It is important to note these rights when they are issued, as they may be difficult to determine retroactively.

B.2.4   End-user type

- **Commercial vs. academic:** There is typically less expensive pricing for academic users than for commercial users. The risk is that academic copies may be purchased in situations that do not qualify.

- **Commercial vs. personal:** Some licences distinguish between commercial use and personal use, charging for the former but not the latter. This is common, for example, with some shareware/freeware packages.

B.2.5   Licence management responsibility

- **Vendor-Managed Usage (VMU):** Technical Licence Management products are in place with some software manufacturers. In these cases, end users can be largely absolved of the Licence-Management aspect of SAM, although it may still be desirable as a check on the correctness of software manufacturer measurements, and to facilitate strategic planning.

- **Customer-Managed Usage (CMU):** Most Licence Management requires customer management, and that is the focus of this guide.

B.2.6   Other

- **Suite:** A group of applications sold together. The terms of the licence normally precludes the individual applications being separated and used individually on separate devices, or by different users simultaneously.

- **Secondary usage:** A licence that provides for the use of software either by secondary users or in a secondary location. Examples are the ability to use one licence on a desktop and a laptop, or on both a work computer and a home computer. Secondary usage rights may come with the main licence, or may be sold separately.

- **Locked licence:** This requires an activation key and is not readily copied or moved.

- **Token-activated:** This uses a dongle or security device to restrict usage.

- **Serialised licence:** Identifiable by a unique serial number, therefore easier to check authenticity.

B.3   Types of licences by sales channel

Frequently there are differences in licence terms and conditions depending on the sales channel. In particular:

- **OEM:** Original equipment manufacturers often have their own licensing terms for software that they supply together with equipment. One of the most significant conditions typically attached to such software is that the software can only be used on the original equipment. If the equipment is replaced, the software cannot be moved to a new machine (although any upgrades used may be movable). The End-User Licence Agreement (EULA) for OEM software is normally between the equipment manufacturer and the end-user, and not between the software manufacturer and the end-user.

- **Retail:** Software sold in retail packaging is the closest to a typical hardware product in terms of physical characteristics. It is also usually the most expensive, and maintaining the proof of licence is typically the most onerous for this type of product.

- **Low volume:** There are low-volume methods of purchasing software licences that do not require the signing of a contract with the software manufacturer, but which usually require user registration. Media may have to be purchased separately. There may be some limited audit rights associated with such licences.

- **High volume:** The high-volume methods of purchasing software licences generally require a signed contract with the software manufacturer. There are typically several levels of contract and/or pricing. This type of contract typically gives the software manufacturer significant audit rights.

- **Service provider:** Software is increasingly being made available through hosting organisations, or Application Service Providers (ASPs). This is normally on a rental or other temporary rights basis.

- **Solution provider:** Software and sometimes hardware from multiple manufacturers may be bundled by a 'solution provider' as a turn-key package. These may be small packages, to major ERP systems. These bundled licences need to be recognised as part of overall SAM Management.

- **Shareware, freeware and public domain software**: These tend to be distributed through the Internet rather than through commercial resellers. There may be many shareware, freeware and public domain software packages in use within an organisation, e.g. zipping utilities. These types of software should be subject to the same controls as software procured from major software manufacturers.

- Shareware: Users are encouraged to copy the program for preview purposes. If the user intends to keep using it then a licence fee must be paid to the developer.
- Freeware: No licence fee is paid but these programs still come with a licence agreement that could potentially be violated. See also 'Open-source' below.
- Public domain: This must be clearly marked as such, and means the copyright holder has relinquished all rights to the software so it can be freely copied, modified, enhanced, etc.

- **Open-source:** This is an increasingly common version of freeware that, as a condition of its licence, requires the source code to be provided and to be modifiable. The licences themselves are free, but there may be charges for media and distribution.

B.4   Counterfeits

Counterfeit software is software that falsely appears to be genuine including its related proof of licence materials. This is not the same as pirated software, as with 'hard-disk loading', whereby a dealer may load unlicensed copies of legitimate software onto machines it sells. With 'hard-disk loading', there are typically no materials supplied which purport to come from the software manufacturer.

There is a serious risk of an organisation purchasing counterfeit software. This risk is greater than many organisations realise because of the sophistication of counterfeiters, and the lack of attention that may be paid by some resellers and end-user organisations to this issue. The risks of using counterfeit software include:

- not being licensed for the software being used

- loss of money spent on the counterfeit software (rather than an apparent saving)

- being in violation of copyright and trademark legislation through possession of the counterfeit products.

The main factors for increased risk of counterfeit software are:

- **Status of suppliers and source of product:** For some software manufacturers and some licensing programs, software may be purchased directly from the manufacturers or from authorised resellers. There is no real risk of purchasing counterfeit products directly from the manufacturer, and a significantly reduced risk from an authorised reseller. A reseller with no special status, selling goods that purport to come from the 'grey market', may involve significantly more risk. 'Grey market' products in particular are at high risk of being counterfeit, because this is a common way of a reseller trying to explain the low cost of counterfeit products.

- **Length of distribution chain:** Collateral or proof of licence received directly from a software manufacturer is the best guarantee of authenticity. The more tiers there are in the distribution channel between the software manufacturer and the end customer, the greater the risk of counterfeit product entering the chain.

- **Size of reseller:** Larger resellers usually are more established, and have more to lose being caught selling counterfeit product. They should take extra measures to ensure they are dealing only with genuine product. Smaller resellers may be more susceptible to selling counterfeit software, knowingly or unknowingly.

- **Geographical location:** If the transaction is based in a country with less stringent copyright/trademark laws or enforcement, the risk of counterfeit software increases.

These risk factors are for awareness only – they are not absolute. There are resellers selling genuine product who are small, at the end of long distribution chains, and based in countries with weak intellectual property protection. Nevertheless, the buyer has a particular duty of care to ensure that the product is genuine with increased risk factors.

It is not possible to give definitive guidance here about how to identify counterfeits. However, the following guidelines are suggested:

- Assess the likelihood of counterfeit product based on the risk factors involved (see above).

- Be knowledgeable about each software manufacturer's security features designed to fight counterfeiting. Descriptions of these may typically be found on software manufacturers' websites.

- Make it clear to your resellers in advance that you will check for the authenticity of the product supplied, especially if the price looks particularly low.

- Review all software collateral received for relevant security features, with a degree of attention corresponding to the risk factors involved.

- Refer to the software manufacturer directly in cases of doubt.

B.5   What is 'proof of licence'?

'Proof of licence' is what a court will accept as proof of a legal entity having a licence. However, it should rarely be necessary to resort to court. Each software manufacturer in general states the requirements for their proof of licence, so no hard and fast rules can be given here. As a general principle, proof of licence requires some form of evidence directly from the software manufacturer. Evidence of payments made to a reseller, or licence confirmations produced by a reseller, will not normally constitute acceptable proof of licence. The spectrum of types of evidence for having a licence includes the following, of which the first three are usually the most important:

- Printed licence confirmation documents from software manufacturers (with security features).

- Electronic licence confirmation documents from software manufacturers held on controlled-access websites.

- Certificates of Authenticity (COAs) are typically engraved, or with other security features. These may be:
  - loose pieces of paper
  - pieces of paper pasted onto manual covers
  - labels glued onto equipment
  - labels printed or glued on retail boxes

  Although COAs are important, backup collateral is often required, because under some circumstances a COA may be attached to an illegal/counterfeit copy, e.g. an unlabelled COA for a less expensive product repackaged with a counterfeit more expensive product.

- Media (CDs, disks, DVDs, plus associated jewel case boxes often with serial numbers, especially for retail products).

- Documentation (especially for older retail products).

- Volume purchasing contracts.

- Purchasing records or analyses provided by software manufacturers, including proof of payment.

- Free-standing letters or other documentation from software manufacturers confirming a grant of licences.

- Invoices from resellers, including proof of payment.

- Sales documentation. It may be desirable to keep copies of sales documentation, e.g. product brochures, to clarify the licences that are included with specific packaged products, e.g. OEM products. The descriptions given on invoices in such cases are often insufficient to clarify what licences are included. In the absence of other stronger documentation, this may be important in helping to establish licence ownership.

Example of contractual definition of proof of volume licences

'This agreement, the applicable enrollment, the enrolled affiliate's order confirmation ... together with proof of payment, will be the enrolled affiliate's evidence of all licences obtained under its enrollment.'

It is important to emphasise that a 'licence confirmation' document produced by a reseller is normally not an acceptable proof of licence, regardless of how impressive it may seem, sometimes with its own security features. Such documents have been produced by many resellers for a number of reasons, such as the delays in customers getting software manufacturer confirmations, and the consolidation of reporting that may occur in software manufacturer confirmations. However, they are not proof of licence, and may create significant legal and financial exposures.

'End-User Licence Agreement' (EULA) is another term that is often used in licensing, especially for retail products. The EULA should be retained just as contracts are retained. Its main purpose is to document the terms and conditions of a licence. It is typically provided in soft copy, or in a printed format without any security features. It generally does not provide proof of licence unless it has security features.

The simple rule to follow is to check with the software vendor directly about what they require you to retain. You may well want to renegotiate on this if you feel the administrative tasks would be onerous. Any such 'special dispensations' should be obtained from the vendor in writing.

B.6   Physical management of software licences

There are a number of challenges associated with the physical management of licences:

- **Varied physical characteristics:** The different types of collateral that can constitute proof of licence have a wide variety of forms and storage characteristics.

- **High risk of loss:** There is a high risk of loss of many types of proof of licence, especially in decentralised environments.

- **Risk of holding counterfeit licences:** See Section B.4.

- **Implementing an effective physical management system:** There need to be separate systems for physical storage, and for recording what is in physical storage (similar to the difference between a warehouse, and the stock control records for the warehouse).

- **Linking multiple licences to determine 'effective' licences:** One current 'effective' licence may require many prior purchases. For example, a single effective licence may be the result of a series of upgrades on an earlier product, and the documentation needs to be retained and linked to show how they build on each other. The associated risk is that of double counting of licences, i.e. that all of these documents will be considered individual licences and totalled, rather than considered together as contractually required. There is also a risk of double-counting licences when there are multiple forms of support, e.g. certificates of authenticity and invoices.

B.6.1   Physical characteristics

Some types of proof of licence are easy to store in traditional filing systems, most notably printed 'volume licensing confirmations'. However, the majority of types of documentation are more difficult to store. In particular:

- **OEM operating system licences:** Most OEM operating system Certificates of Authenticity are now physically fixed to a PC, and cannot be removed without effectively destroying them. There is no option for separate physical storage of this document, and it can be controlled only in a database. Barcode readers may be used to capture the relevant information.

- **Electronic Confirmations:** Many software manufacturer volume licence confirmation documents now are purely electronic. While the on-line copy is definitive, it is prudent to print a copy and treat the printout as if it were a hard-copy original licence confirmation, for ease of reference and as backup for the electronic on-line versions.

- **Media:** This is primarily an issue for older software, or where current licences are based on upgrades from older licences where media formed part of the proof of licence. As an example, a company may have purchased large quantities of software via a non-volume channel, so that there is a CD to keep with each. There may have been successive upgrades, including to competitive products, but the original CD is still part of the proof of original licence on which all successive upgrades are based.

- **Manuals:** This is also primarily an issue for older software, especially for some software where the certificates of authenticity were pasted to manual covers. If the manuals were given to end users, the certificates were likely to be lost. However, keeping them centrally in manual form was also problematical. One solution practised by some organisations was to rip off and store the covers with their certificates, and throw away the manuals.

If you have a large quantity of bulky support collateral for early licences, such as CDs, it is worth asking the software manufacturer of your latest licences if they will accept in writing as valid a certificate of destruction from a recognised destruction agent, citing relevant details of the materials destroyed. However, there have been situations where software manufacturers have refused to allow the destruction of CDs even though they were very old.

B.6.2   High risk of loss

There is a high risk of loss of physical licences, especially in decentralised environments where the importance of physical proof of licence is not recognised. This is a significant cause of financial loss, when organisations cannot prove the licences that they assume they have purchased and need to repurchase to prove compliance. There is also a heightened risk of loss in centralised environments to a catastrophic event such as a fire. To minimise these risks, a centralised approach is most appropriate, with off-site backup copies of licence inventory records kept against the risk of catastrophic events.

B.6.3   Implementing an effective physical management system

The physical management system for licences may be just a filing cabinet in a very small organisation, but for most organisations this will not be sufficient. There should be two separate parts to the system, namely a storage system for physical documents and other evidence, and an inventory system to record what is there. Again, in small organisations, the inventory may be kept simply in a spreadsheet, but this will typically be inadequate. What is recommended is a Document Management system that can keep scanned copies of all physical documents. The physical documents can then be filed away securely without any need for normal access, with reliance placed instead on the scanned images.

Some documentation that legally may form part of the proof of licence, should already be covered by other Document Management systems, e.g. invoices and contracts. Depending on the functionality of the relevant systems, there may be no need to do anything further. Alternatively, it may be preferable for practical reasons to include copies of such documentation in the licensing Document Management system. For example, it is sometimes difficult for organisations to retrieve back copies of invoices when they are needed several years later, after system changes or archiving.

B.7   Other common licensing problems

Any of the issues discussed in this Appendix may represent a problem. However, the following are some common problem areas encountered not already specifically discussed:

- **Software licensing for sub-contractors/agents:** It should be clear when contractors are employed who is responsible for which licences. Typically, the organisation will be responsible for any software it installs on the contractor's machines, and for relevant licences, etc.

- **Software licensing for partially owned subsidiaries:** Volume licensing agreements may have conditions concerning which entities may purchase under the agreements. It is a common problem that these terms may be breached by providing software to affiliates which do not qualify.

APPENDIX C CONSIDERATIONS IN SELECTING SAM TOOLS

This Appendix supports Chapter 7 'Tools and Technology' with which it should be read. The principal objective of using a tool should be to automate a process to make its operation as efficient as possible.

C.1 General points of consideration

The following is a sample list of best practice requirements that organisations should consider when evaluating the functional abilities of SAM tools:

- A careful definition and evaluation of tool requirements has been performed before selection (Statement of Requirements (SoR)).

- All the mandatory and desirable functional tool requirements are based on a defined ICT process:
  - all mandatory requirements covered
  - the tool provides a minimum of 80% compliance for all operational requirements
  - the tool does not require extensive tailoring or product customisation
    the tool supports the SAM processes and is also compliant with ITIL and BS 15000 principles
  - the tool satisfies current and future business requirements.

- The tool conforms with overall technology and management architectures, policies and strategies.

- The tool provides the required interfaces with Systems Management tools.

- The tool provides the required interfaces with business process such as HR, financial, and research and development.

Some points that organisations should consider when evaluating the functionality of a SAM tool:

- data structure, data handling and integration

- integration of multi-vendor infrastructure components, and the need to absorb new components in the future – these will place particular demands on the data handling and modelling capabilities of the tool

- conformity to international open standards

- integration with other existing management tools

- flexibility in implementation, usage and data sharing

- usability – the ease of use permitted by the user interface

- support for monitoring service levels – response and resolution

- distributed clients with a centralised shared database (e.g. client server)

- conversion, import and export requirements for previously tracked data

- data backup, integrity, control and security

- support options provided by the tool vendor

- organisational constraints:
    - impact on the organisation
    - staff availability, experience and skill sets
- implementation complexity
- role-based access control (for corporate organisations that allow different access levels for different roles and levels)
- costs:
    - software/hardware (purchase and installation)
    - licences/training/development and customisation
    - consulting.

C.2   Practical guidelines for the selection of SAM tools

Consideration must be given to the exact requirements of the tool. What are the mandatory requirements and what are the desired requirements? Some practical guidelines are listed here:

- A correct balance needs to be struck between defining an organisation's own requirements for SAM, and possibly modifying those requirements to fit existing tool capabilities. In theory, tools should be modified if necessary to meet an organisation's own requirements. In practice, however, SAM requirements should not be so unique that each organisation needs extensive customisation to meet them. Therefore, requirements should still be carefully defined, and existing tools assessed against those requirements. There should be existing tools that meet most of those requirements. If not, then the organisation should seriously review its stated requirements to see if they are realistic, rather than immediately going for a custom solution.

- It is essential to have an SoR for use during the selection process This statement can be used as a 'tick list'. The requirements can be rated in terms of mandatory facilities, needed facilities and 'nice to have' facilities.

- The tool must be adequately flexible to support the required access rights. You must be able to determine who is permitted to access what data and for what purpose, e.g. read access to customers.

- In the early stages consideration must also be given to the platform on which the tool will be expected to operate – this may be on existing hardware and software or a new purchase. There may be restrictions laid down by ICT Strategy, for example, all new products may have to reside on specific servers. This would restrict which products that could be included in the evaluation process.

- Make sure that the procurement fits within existing approved budgets.

- There are many SAM tools available. Don't restrict your choice to the one(s) the organisation knows about. Surf the Web, look at SAM publications, ask other organisations, ask consultants or talk to industry forum(s) to see what products are available. There may be a user group for the product – if there is, talk to the chairperson, as this may lead to useful feedback.

- During the early stages of the vetting process, think about vendor and tool credibility. Are they still going to be supporting the purchase in a few months or a year's time? Consider the past record of the supplier as well as that of the tool. Telephone the supplier Service Desk to see how easy it is to get through, and ask some test questions to assess technical competence.

- Ask the vendor to arrange a visit to a reference site to see what their experience is with the tool in practice – if possible without the vendor or supplier present. Make sure that the organisation has similar requirements of the tool. See the tool in operation and speak to the users about their experiences, both initially and ongoing.

- Don't limit your requirements to functionality. Ask about the product's ability to perform, enlarge the size of the databases, recover from failure and maintain data integrity. Does the product conform to international standards? Is it efficient enough to enable you to meet your Service Level Requirements (SLR)?

- Verify the tools chosen for ease of deployment and ensure there are no detrimental effects on the functioning of the system.

- Assess the management reports generated by the tool. In some tools, the generation of meaningful reports can be a cumbersome and time-consuming task. To monitor the output of the processes, the tool should have many methods of aggregating the data in meaningful and, for the business, understandable ways.

- Assess the training needs of the organisation and evaluate the capability of the supplier to provide the appropriate training. In particular, consider training costs, training location, time required and how soon after training the tool will be in use. During the implementation process, ensure that sufficient training is provided – think about how the new tool will impact both ICT and customer.

Ensure that interfaces with other tools and telephony are functioning correctly. It is wise to identify whether the planned combination has been used (or tried) elsewhere, and with what results. Consider parallel running before finally going live.

Verify the project by running a pilot to ensure reporting structures and data capture meet the objectives and requirements of SAM.

A much more detailed evaluation must now be completed. Demonstrations of the products need to be arranged. Ensure that all relevant members of staff are involved. Be wary of demonstrations – always see the live product in operation. If possible, provide the test data and assess the provided results against expectations. Be cautious of being promised things in the next release. Use a reference site to confirm impressions from the demonstration. Use the SoR and adjust the 'tick list' during the demonstrations of the products. Refer to this later to assist in reducing the shortlist to the final chosen product.

The work obviously doesn't end when the product has been selected. In many ways, this could be considered as only the beginning. The tool now has to be implemented. Once the hardware platform has been prepared, and the software loaded, data population needs to be considered. What, where from, how and when? Timing is important to the implementation, testing and finally going live processes. Resources must be available to ensure success. In other words, don't schedule during a known busy period, such as year-end processing.

Following live implementation, hold regular meetings with both ICT and customers to ensure the agreed benefits have been realised. Some aspects may have to be refined. During this process, also consider the performance of the supplier. If they have not performed to your expectations, they should be managed and advised (in writing) as soon as possible.

APPENDIX D POSSIBLE SAM DATABASE CONTENTS

This Appendix gives suggestions for the possible physical storage contents and corresponding electronic databases for SAM. See Figure 7.1 in Chapter 7: 'Tools and Technology' for how these relate to SAM overall, and to the ITIL concepts of the Definitive Software Library (DSL) and the Configuration Management Database (CMDB).

D.1 Software licence inventory

Table D.1 – Licence information and inventory

Field type	Comments
CMDB Configuration Item (CI) attributes	These are the types of attributes for identification of a CI within the CMDB, additional to the detailed fields below. Further information is given in Annex 7C of the ITIL *Guide to Service Support*.
	• CI name
	• copy or serial number
	• category (e.g. software, documentation, media)
	• type (amplifying information to category, e.g. program module)
	• owner responsible
	• responsibility date (that the owner became responsible)
	• accepted date (satisfactorily tested)
	• parent CI relationships (not already included below)
	• child CI relationships (not already included below)
	• other CI relationships (not already included below)
	• Request for Change (RFC) numbers affecting this CI
	• change records affecting this CI
	• problem records affecting this CI
	• incident records affecting this CI.
Summary control information	
Licence status and counts	Licence status and use counts for each status (especially for volume licences). Status can be:
	• current effective licence – used
	• current effective licence – unused
	• subsumed licence (e.g. a later upgrade licence is based on it)
	• disposed licence (e.g. transferred in part to demerged units).

Field type	Comments
Summary control information	
Where used	Link(s) to where the licence is used. This depends on the type of licensing, but could be: • specific PC • specific server and/or processor • named person • named site.
Exception flags	Multiple flags possible, for example: • underlying licence not identified for upgrade licence • full proof of licence not yet located • licence not yet reported – periodic reporting required.
Cost	Original cost, current depreciated cost plus currency name.
Cost-centre	Currently assigned cost-centre.
Basic reference information	
Licence number	Unique licence reference number, e.g. from software manufacturer's licence confirmation document (as opposed to the reseller confirmation document).
Reseller confirmation document	Unique confirmation document reference number as provided by a reseller.
Ordered product	Description of product
Ordered version	
Ordered quantity	
Software manufacturer	
Software manufacturer part number	
Platform	Hardware or specific operating system under which the software runs.
Licensor	Normally the software manufacturer, but could be the OEM, a system integrator, etc.
Licensing programme	For example, retail, OEM, various volume licensing programmes.
Volume licensing programme programme reference	Contract reference if obtained through a volume licensing.

Field type	Comments
Basic reference information	
PO number	
PO date	
Reseller	
Reseller part number	Is often different from software manufacturer part number, and may be needed to reconcile to reseller invoices and reports.
Invoice number	
Invoice date	
Country of usage reported	Country in which the software will be used, as required for some software manufacturer volume reporting.
Ordering location as shown by software manufacturer	Ordering location or entity as recorded by software manufacturer, for the purpose of reconciling internal records to software manufacturer confirmations and records.
Ordering location as shown by reseller	Ordering location or entity as recorded by reseller, for the purpose of reconciling internal records to reseller reports and records.
Proof of licence	Cross reference(s) to specific documentation that provides proof of licence, and where it is physically located.
Media	Cross reference(s) to media provided with licence, if relevant.
Documentation	Cross reference(s) to documentation provided with licence, if relevant.
Product components	For products that consist of a suite of other products, a list of those components to facilitate identification and linking.
Current entitlement of original licence purchased	
Product	
Version	
Basis for enhanced entitlement and cross reference	The specified licence may have a different product entitlement from the name given on the initial order. Possible reasons include: • upgrade insurance • technology guarantees • other software manufacturer announcements.

Field type	Comments
Terms and conditions	
Source references	Cross reference(s) to specific documentation of licensing terms and conditions.
Licensing basis	For example, per PC, per device, per user, total number of users (concurrent use), per mailbox, per five printers, per location, per subsidiary, per organisation.
Expiry date	N/A for permanent licences, valid date e.g. for upgrade insurance or for rental licences.
Product substitution rights	For example, downgrade rights, language version substitution rights.
Secondary rights	For example, home-use rights, joint desktop and laptop rights.
Transferability	For example: • freely transferable (e.g. retail products) • transferable only together with hardware (e.g. most OEM products) • individual counts transferable only within purchasing entity, entire licence freely transferable (e.g. some low-end volume licences) • individual counts transferable within affiliate companies, external transfers subject to restrictions (e.g. some high-end volume licences).
External licence transfer requirements	For example: • formal documentation required? • software manufacturer notification required?
Linkages	
Upgrades from	Linkages to the underlying licences which this licence is upgrading.
Upgrades to	Linkages to the subsequent licences which upgrade this licence.
Secondary use	Linkages between licences if separate licences are required for primary and secondary use, e.g. for home use.
Upgrade insurance details (where applicable)	
Period	Beginning and end dates during which insurance is applicable.
Notice date(s)	Dates when notice must be given to extend, or to cancel automatic renewal.

D.2   Installed software inventory

Table D.2 – Inventory of installed software

Field type	Comments
CMDB Configuration Item (CI) attributes	See previous section for explanation
Summary control information	
Installation status	For example, full/partial
Licence used	Link to licence to cover this usage, or N/A if no licence required (e.g. internally developed applications)
Exception flags	Multiple flags possible, e.g.: • apparently unlicensed installation • apparently incomplete de-installation.
Basic reference information	
Product	
Version	
Updates installed	Updates for the current version of the software, not new versions.
Security patches installed	
Hardware on which installed	
Country of usage	Country in which software is actually being used, as required for some software manufacturer reporting. May also be important to help track licence compliance on a country-by-country basis for dealing with local authorities.
Cost-centre of hardware owner	
Date of last discovery	
Metrics	Metrics used for identifying software.
Date first discovered	

D.3   Source documentation

The following types of physical documentation will generally need to be filed. It is recommended that copies be scanned and filed in an electronic Document Management system, if possible, to ensure better availability of the information as well as greater security for the source documents.

An indexing system will be needed to allow cross-referencing from different databases.

Some documentation is now available electronically (e.g. some software manufacturer licence confirmations, terms and conditions documents, general licensing information). These electronic documents generally should be included in the same filing system as similar types of physical documents.

Table D.3 – Filing of documentation

Documentation type	Examples
Contracts	Contracts plus amendments – with software manufacturers (master agreements, etc.), resellers, outsourcers.
SLAs	With internal units and with outsourcers.
Terms and conditions	Various formats. Volume licensing versions may be updated periodically and downloaded electronically.
Proof of licence documentation	Licence confirmations, copies of invoices, and any other documentation required not already included in the filing system. See Chapter 5 and Appendix B for further discussion.
Price lists	
Copies of other relevant internal transaction documentation, if not readily available from alternative systems	Examples are: • copies of internal orders placed • copies of work/installation orders • copies of purchase orders placed.
Purchase record downloads	From software manufacturers, resellers.
Correspondence	With resellers, software manufacturers, etc.
Licensing programme descriptions	From software manufacturers.
Licensing explanations	From software manufacturers.

D.4   Working documentation

It will generally be desirable to file the following types of physical working documentation formally. (Some of this will be in electronic format.)

Table D.4 – Filing of documentation

Documentation type	Examples
Compliance process documentation	Documentation of the results of compliance processes as described in Section 5.4. These include: • periodic licence compliance reconciliations • verification and audit checks (and problem analysis of cause of discrepancies) • security compliance (e.g. completeness and timeliness of security patch installation, and problem analysis of cause of discrepancies) • other policy and procedure compliance.
Process improvement reviews	

D.5   Media

There needs to be inventory control over physical media as well as over distribution copies of software which often may be located on servers. Some specific organisational approaches are recommended by software manufacturers for their own volume licensing media.

D.6   Guidance documentation

It will generally be desirable to file copies of SAM guidance documentation from all sources, including software manufacturers, resellers, and professional sources (such as for this guide).

D.7   Hardware inventory

It is not in the scope of this guide to cover hardware except for those aspects that are necessary for effective SAM. One of these aspects is the identification of hardware characteristics that affect software licensing. It may be desirable to include flags in hardware inventories to facilitate software licensing calculations. For example:

- if a PC is a qualifying PC for the purposes of site licensing counts
- processing power for licensing which is calculated on this basis
- who owns the machine and is responsible for licensing (in the case of hosters and similar).

APPENDIX E CHOOSING A SAM PARTNER

The list below identifies some criteria worth investigating when selecting a SAM partner. The focus of this Appendix is on choosing a SAM consultant, but much of it can be applied to other types of SAM partners. (See Chapter 8 for a more general discussion of the types of SAM partners and the services they provide).

At present, there is limited depth in the SAM market. Nonetheless, just about every organisation working in any related area will claim to be able to offer SAM consultancy and related services. As the need for SAM emerges, it is anticipated that yet more companies will enter the SAM provider market.

The most critical selection criterion in most cases will probably be the skills and experience of the individuals who will be responsible for the services to be provided, more so than the overall experience of the organisation for which they work, although both are important.

There is probably no perfect partner, and it may be appropriate to have more than one partner working together. At least one partner should probably have extensive and practical current licensing knowledge, such as a good reseller should have.

Table E.1 – Importance criteria for potential SAM partners

Key to importance weighting – Low, Medium, High (L, M, H)

Ref	Criteria	Import-ance	Comments
	Qualifications and capabilities of the organisation		
1	Can the organisation demonstrate experience for the type of assistance sought?	H	
2	Does the organisation have established methodologies and tools for the type of assistance sought?	H	
3	How long has the organisation been providing the type of assistance sought?	M	
4	What quality of licensing expertise is expected to be applied as part of the service to be provided – examine details of people, training and qualifications, and length of time in jobs.	H	This is generally one of the most important issues in the selection of a potential partner. The expertise needs to be realistically available and applied to the work without having to make exceptional requests.
5	If the service requires determination of effective licensing, what relevant tools and methodologies can be demonstrated?	H	One of the most complex issues in licence compliance is the determination of current effective licences taking into account all past licence purchases including full and upgrade products of various types, upgrade insurance

Ref	Criteria	Import-ance	Comments
Qualifications and capabilities of the organisation			
			and its timing relative to release dates of new versions, and detailed contractual issues about how previous licences relate to site licences, or are they separate and available for redeployment).
6	Does the organisation offer other related services that may complement the type of assistance currently sought?	L	May create synergies, but also may create conflicts of interest – see below.
7	Where is the service available geographically?	L	More important for multinational organisations.
8	In what languages is the service available?	L	More important for multinational organisations.
9	How old is the organisation?	L	
10	How financially strong is the organisation?	M	More important for organisations where there may need to be a long-term relationship, e.g. with tool vendors or outsourcers.
SAM focus			
11	How many people does the organisation have, globally and locally, dedicated 100% to providing SAM-type services (not full-time equivalents of people doing other work as well)	M	This is a good indicator of the seriousness of an organisation about SAM.
12	Are SAM services provided by a dedicated unit or out of a more generalist unit?	M	This is a good indicator of the seriousness of an organisation about SAM.
Conflicts of interest			
13	Is the organisation primarily dependent on a particular manufacturer for most of its work?	M	A close relationship with a particular software manufacturer can be an advantage in terms of detailed knowledge of that software manufacturer's products, but needs to be assessed against the possible conflicts of interest involved, e.g. advocating that software manufacturer's products, inappropriately or leaking confidential information back to that software manufacturer.

Ref	Criteria	Import-ance	Comments
Conflicts of interest			
14	Does the organisation have vested interests in other areas that might affect the independence of its SAM services, e.g. selling licences, selling and/or installing SAM tools, or providing outsourcing services?	M	Involvement in any of these areas can be an advantage because of the additional knowledge it gives to the organisation, but needs to be assessed against the possible conflicts of interest involved.
15	Does the organisation offer its services on a fee basis rather than related to the sale of other products?	M	Fee-based services are generally preferable from an independence point of view.
16	Does it appear that the service is being offered as a 'loss-leader' with the objective of cross-selling other services in the future, e.g. as a result of knowing more about internal ICT plans?	H	Loss-leaders may represent false savings. The provider will typically not be able to justify the quality-in-depth that the job requires, and the work may be biased to ensure the creation of new revenue opportunities.
Qualifications and capabilities of the principal individuals proposed			
17	Does the individual have demonstrated experience for the type of assistance sought? Over what period?	H	Very important.
18	Can the individual answer relevant detailed questions without research during initial discussions?	H	Proof of capabilities.
19	Does the individual have qualifications for the type of assistance sought? For example, licensing certifications from software manufacturers.	M	
References			
20	Can you talk privately to at least two references for whom the organisation has previously provided similar services, and get good feedback?	H	Very important.
Other questions			
21	How well does the organisation control its own software assets? Ask to see a live demonstration and talk to real end users.	M	Demonstrates how serious the organisation is about SAM.

Ref	Criteria	Import-ance	Comments
Other questions			
22	Does the organisation have any other general certifications or qualifications, e.g. ISO certification or software manufacturer certifications?	L	The question is how relevant the certifications are to the services being requested.

APPENDIX F THE DETAILED CONTENTS OF A SAM BUSINESS CASE

A business case for the implementation of SAM should contain, where appropriate:

- identification and quantification of all of the benefits to the business and its customers
- the overall scope, size of the task, objectives, deliverables, impacts, CSFs, KPIs, and business benefits of the proposed solution
- the business sponsor/owner and the stakeholders
- a description of the current situation, including strengths, weaknesses, opportunities and threats
- the strategic fit and details of how the preferred solution conforms to, supports or deviates from existing corporate, business and ICT initiatives, policies, strategies and plans
- details of how these key strategic objectives and benefits will be achieved
- the implications, risks and impacts of not proceeding with the business case (do nothing)
- a description of the proposed new processes and their objectives
- details of all constraints and dependencies
- the level of authorisation or approval necessary and the required timescale for approval
- industry considerations:
  - external opportunities and threats, market share and competitors, present and forecasted volumes, regulatory and legislative constraints, trends in pricing, quality, standards and technology, competitive services and products, their quality and performance
- details of how the objectives, deliverables, CSFs and business benefits will be monitored and measured, including operational targets
- details of the Project Management methods and approach
- identification and quantification of all risks:
  - description, probability, impact and analysis of the risk, steps taken to manage and minimise the risk, any necessary mitigating countermeasures and expenditure
- the preferred solution with its advantages, disadvantages, benefits, risks, costs, resources and timescales, including ongoing requirements and costs
- alternative solutions considered and their advantages, disadvantages, benefits, risks, costs and timescales, including ongoing requirements and costs, including the 'do nothing' option
- the reasons for selecting any preferred suppliers and rejecting alternative suppliers
- details of key milestones in the implementation process and overall dependencies
- details of parent programmes or projects and their interfaces and approval status
- details of any dependent programmes or projects and their dependencies and approval status
- the authorising, owning or sponsoring body and budget(s) to be used

- details of the approach to be adopted (e.g. in-house resources, contracted-in resources or managed service)
- procurement plans and policies with details of preferred suppliers and their costs and comparative alternatives and their costs
- financial analysis:
  - financial assumptions, initial costs, ongoing costs, financial constraints and budgets, payback period and ROI, tolerances and sensitivities, funding and stakeholders, the possible effects on the organisation's financial performance and profitability
- the requirements for external resources and finances from other departments and organisations
- contractual, legal and regulatory issues
- environmental issues
- clear, concise and unambiguous summary and recommendations.

APPENDIX G EXAMPLE CONTENTS OF A SOFTWARE POLICY

An organisational software policy should address:

- the use and misuse of ICT systems including hardware and software
- software use, licensing and copyright policy
- the use of personal software
- the use of shareware and freeware
- the use of illegal or pirated software
- the requesting and procurement of software, including the business justification and the registration of requests for new or enhanced software
- the software procurement approval process
- defined ownership, roles and responsibilities for enforcement, administration and non-compliance
- the use of SAM processes and procedures
- the downloading of software
- the use of the Internet and e-mail systems
- the copying of software
- the software selection and evaluation process
- the selection of software resellers, suppliers and manufacturers, including a preferred list of suppliers
- a common software distribution and upgrade process
- protection of the organisation's own intellectual property
- sign-off and acceptance of the software policy by all personnel including all new employees and all contractors
- responsibilities (by role, not individual) for ownership and monitoring of processes and data
- methods of disseminating the software policy and any amendments.

The remainder of this appendix contains an example policy document that could be used to develop an organisation's hardware and software policy.

G.1 Sample policy on the use of hardware and software

All ICT resources, including all hardware, software and network systems, provided by the company are to be used only for company business. Use of the company's ICT resources implies that you:

- assume responsibility for their appropriate use
- agree to abide by this policy
- agree to abide by all national and local laws and regulations
- agree to abide by all software contractual terms and conditions.

All software and hardware purchased for or developed by company employees or persons acting on their behalf will remain the intellectual property of the company and must be used in compliance with all company policies, relevant licences and contractual terms and conditions.

No equipment from outside the company should be used within company premises or connected to the company network without the prior written consent of the IS department.

All employees are responsible for reading and complying with all conditions applying to the proper use of company hardware and software.

All software and hardware will be purchased through the IS department to ensure that cost-effective and efficient systems are purchase to corporate standards. All requests for software or hardware should be submitted to IS on the company standard IS request form.

The standard company configurations are documented on the company intranet at ....

These configurations will be fully supported by the IS department. Employees needing configurations or components other than these should submit a standard request with the accompanying justification.

Any violation or contravention of this policy will result in specific action being initiated against the instigator. This will consist of:

- disciplinary action as stated within the company's employee handbook
- civil or criminal proceedings where appropriate.

G.2   Acknowledgement of hardware/software policy

This form is used to acknowledge receipt and understanding of and compliance with the company's policy on the use of IS hardware and software. The form should be completed using the following steps:

- read and study the company policy on the use of hardware and software
- complete and sign the form and return it to IS administration.

I have read a copy of the company policy on the use of hardware and software and I understand and agree to the following:

- the terms and conditions contained within the policy document

- that any hardware and software components provided by the company for my use will remain the property of the company

- that I will make reasonable efforts to protect all components and information provided by the company from theft, damage or corruption

- that I will not add, modify, change or upgrade any of the software or hardware components provided by the company for my use without the prior written permission of the IS department

- that I will not copy or duplicate any of the software components provided, or allow any of the components provided to be copied by anyone else

- that if I leave the company all computer materials, including all hardware, software and information received from the company will be returned prior to my departure

- that no software will be purchased or downloaded from the Internet and installed on any of the equipment received from the company without the prior written permission of the IS department.

Employee name: _____

Employee title: _____

Department: _____

Post: _____

Location: _____

Employee signature: _____

Date: _____

INDEX

W

Other Information Sources and Services

The IT Service Management Forum (itSMF)

The IT Service Management Forum Ltd (itSMF) is the only internationally recognised and independent body dedicated to IT Service Management. It is a not-for-profit organisation, wholly owned, and principally operated, by its membership.

The itSMF is a major influence on, and contributor to, Industry Best Practice and Standards worldwide, working in partnership with OGC (the owners of ITIL), the British Standards Institution (BSI), the Information Systems Examination Board (ISEB) and the Examination Institute of the Netherlands (EXIN).

Founded in the UK in 1991, there are now a number of chapters around the world with new ones seeking to join all the time. There are well in excess of 1000 organisations covering over 10,000 individuals represented in the membership. Organisations range from large multi-nationals such as AXA, GuinnessUDV, HP, Microsoft and Procter & Gamble in all market sectors, through central & local bodies, to independent consultants.

How to contact us:

The IT Service Management Forum Ltd
Webbs Court
8 Holmes Road
Farley
Reading RG6 7BH
Tel: +44 (0) 118 926 0888
Fax: +44 (0) 118 926 3073
Email: service@itsmf.com
or visit our web-site at:
www.itsmf.com

ITIL training and professional qualifications

There are currently two examining bodies offering equivalent qualifications: ISEB (The Information Systems Examining Board), part of the British Computer Society, and Stitching EXIN (The Netherlands Examinations Institute). Jointly with OGC and itSMF (the IT Service Management Forum), they work to ensure that a common standard is adopted for qualifications worldwide. The syllabus is based on the core elements of ITIL and complies with ISO9001 Quality Standard. Both ISEB and EXIN also accredit training organisations to deliver programmes leading to qualifications.

For further information:

visit ISEB's web-site at:
www.bcs.org.uk

and EXIN:
www.exin.nl

Best Practice:
the OGC approach with ITIL and PRINCE2

OGC Best Practice is an approach to management challenges as well as the application of techniques and actions.

Practical, flexible and adaptable, management guidance from OGC translates the very best of the world's practices into guidance of an internationally recognised standard. Both PRINCE2 and ITIL publications can help every organisation to:

- Run projects more efficiently
- Reduce project risk
- Purchase IT more cost effectively
- Improve organisational Service Delivery.

What is ITIL and why use it?

ITIL's starting point is that organisations do not simply use IT; they depend on it. Managing IT as effectively as possible must therefore be a high priority.

ITIL consists of a unique library of guidance on providing quality IT services. It focuses tightly on the customer, cost effectiveness and building a culture that puts the emphasis on IT performance.

Used by hundreds of the world's most successful organisations, its seven core titles are available in print, online and CD-ROM formats. They are:

- Service Support
- Service Delivery
- Planning to Implement Service Management
- Application Management
- ICT Infrastructure Management
- Security Management
- The Business Perspective
  (Due to publish Summer 2004)

What is PRINCE2 and why use it?

Since its introduction in 1989, PRINCE has been widely adopted by both the public and private sectors and is now recognised as a de facto standard for project management – and for the management of change.

PRINCE2, the most evolved version, is driven by its experts and users to offer control, transparency, focus and ultimate success for any project you need to implement.

Publications are available in various formats: print, online and CD-ROM. Its main titles are:

- Managing Successful Projects with PRINCE2
- People Issues and PRINCE2
- PRINCE2 Pocket Book
- Tailoring PRINCE2
- Business Benefits through Project Management

Other related titles:
- Passing the PRINCE2 Examinations
- Managing Successful Programmes
- Management of Risk – Guidance for Practitioners

Ordering

The full range of ITIL and PRINCE2 publications can be purchased direct via **www.get-best-practice.co.uk** or through calling TSO Customer Services on **0870 600 5522**. Network licences can also be purchased here.

You are also able to subscribe to content online through this website or by calling TSO Customer Services on **0870 600 5522**. For more information on how to subscribe online please refer to our help pages on the website.

Dear customer ■ ■ ■ ■ ■ ■ ■ ■ ■ ■ ■ ■ ■ ■

We would like to hear from you with any comments or suggestions that you have on how we can improve our current products or develop new ones for the ITIL series. Please complete this questionnaire and we will enter you into our quarterly draw. The winner will receive a copy of Software Asset Management worth £35!

1 Personal Details

Name ....

Organisation ....

Job Title ....

Department ....

Address ....

....

Telephone Number ....

Email ....

2 Nature of Organisation (tick one box only)

☐ Consultancy/Training
☐ Computing/IT/Software
☐ Industrial
☐ Central Government
☐ Local Government
☐ Academic/Further education
☐ Private Health
☐ Public Health (NHS)
☐ Finance
☐ Construction
☐ Telecommunications
☐ Utilities
☐ Other (Please specify)

....

3 How did you heard about ITIL?

☐ Work/Colleagues
☐ Internet/Web (please specify)

....

☐ Marketing Literature
☐ itSMF
☐ Other (please specify)

....

4 Where did you purchase this book?

☐ Web – www.tso.co.uk/bookshop
☐ Web – www.get-best-practice.co.uk
☐ Web – Other (please specify)

....

☐ Bookshop (please specify)

....

☐ Training Course
☐ Other (please specify)

....

5 How many people use ITIL in your company?

☐ 1-5
☐ 6-10
☐ 11-50
☐ 51-200
☐ 201+

6 How many people use your copy of this title?

☐ 2-5
☐ 6-10
☐ 11+

7 Overall, how do you rate this title?

☐ Excellent
☐ Very Good
☐ Good
☐ Fair
☐ Poor

8 What do you most like about the book? (tick all that apply)

☐ Ease of use
☐ Well structured
☐ Contents
☐ Index
☐ Hints and tips

9 Do you have any suggestions for improvement?

....

....

....

....

10 How do you use this book? (tick all that apply)

☐ Problem Solver
☐ Reference
☐ Tutorial
☐ Other (please specify)

....

11 Did you know there are 7 core titles in the **ITIL** series?

☐ No
☐ Yes

12 Do you have any other **ITIL** titles?

☐ No
☐ Yes (please specify)

....

13 Do you use the **ITIL** CDs?

☐ No
☐ Yes (please specify)

....

14 Are you aware that most of the **ITIL** series is now available online at www.get-best-practice.co.uk?

☐ Yes
☐ No

15 Do you currently subscribe to any online content found at www.get-best-practice.co.uk?

☐ No
☐ Yes (please specify)

....

16 Did you know that you can network your CDs and Online Subscription, to offer your project managers access to this material at their desktop?

Yes/No

☐ Please tick this box if you require further information.

17 Did you know that you are able to purchase a maintenance agreement for your CD-ROM that will allow you to receive immediately any revised versions, at no additional cost?

Yes/No

☐ Please tick this box if you require further information.

18 What business change guidance/methods does your company use?

☐ PRINCE2
☐ Managing Successful Programmes
☐ Management of Risk
☐ Successful Delivery Toolkit
☐ Business Systems Development (BSD)
☐ Other (please specify)

....

19 What is the job title of the person who makes the decision to implement **ITIL** and/or purchase IT?

....

....

20 Which three websites do you visit the most?

1 ....

2 ....

3 ....

21 Which 3 professional magazines do you read the most?

1 ....

2 ....

3 ....

22 Will you be attending any events or conferences this year related to IT, if so, which?

....

To enter your Questionnaire into our monthly draw please return this form to our Freepost Address:

Marketing – ITIL Questionnaire
TSO
Freepost ANG4748
Norwich
NR3 1YX

The ITIL series is available in a range of formats: hard copy, CD-Rom and now available as an online subscription for further details and to purchase visit www.get-best-practice.co.uk

Any further enquiries or questions about ITIL or the Office of Government Commerce should be directed to the OGC Service Desk:

The OGC Service Desk
Rosebery Court
St Andrews Business Park
Norwich
NR7 0HS

Email: ServiceDesk@ogc.gsi.gov.uk
Telephone: 0845 000 4999